GW01553203

CLOG DANCING

by Brenda Walker

A step-by-step guide to the art of traditional
Durham & Northumberland Clog Dancing

An Introduction for Beginners
progressing to Intermediate

"A legacy of steps" dedicated to my family
and the Walker Family Dancers

ISBN 978 1-904499-20-6

Further copies of this book may be obtained from

www. brendawalker.co.uk

Front cover by Solomon Walker
Illustrations by Robert Olley

First published in United Kingdom of Great Britain in
2007   by Roundtuit Publishing, 32 Cookes Wood,
,Broom Park Durham DH7 7RL

Printed in the United Kingdom of Great Britain by Prontaprint Durham 0191 384 3220.

Acknowledgements

I wish to thank Harry and our children for their continued support and interest in all our dance activities.

My thanks to Don Watson for his enthusiastic support at our events and great knowledge of the history of clog dancing.

Thank you to my wonderful troupe of dancers for their hard work and dedication to perfect the steps of our region to perform at numerous International Festivals around the world.

Finally, my appreciation and thanks to the hundreds of dancers who have attended my classes over the past thirty years and inspired me to compile this collection of steps.

A few words about the author ....

I was born and bred in Newcastle upon Tyne in 1946 and commenced dancing at the age of 8 years. My earliest recollection of dance lessons was attending lessons for Scottish Country dancing with Major A.A. Bourne in Gateshead. As a teenager I was taught Highland dancing in Newcastle by Harry Picken and during my late teens I was taught Irish dancing by John Limer at the Tyneside Irish Folk Dance Society in Gateshead. With this Folk Dance Society I had my first taste of an International Folk Dance Festival and was introduced to clog dancing when I danced a solo clog dance in Dusseldorf for a dancer who was unable to attend a Festival in 1966. It was very exciting and my interest for clog dancing started here.

After having to leave the north-east for four years in 1970 I returned in 1974 with a family, my eldest daughter, Tiffany, and my son, Solomon. I heard there was a clog dancer living in Chester-le-Street and discovered Mary Jameson, Johnson Ellwood's daughter. For the next ten years Mary taught me clog steps she had been taught by her father during which time I opened a school for clog dancing in 1979 which was located in Durham. In 1983, as well as my second daughter, Bridie, arriving on the scene, I started tap dancing and eventually attended the Elsa Wilkins Dance Academy in Sunderland in 1986 after winning the Northern Counties Clog Championship Belt outright. Elsa Wilkins taught me tap dancing for 8 years and in 1994 I acquired a Fellowship in tap dancing with the International Dance Teachers' Association.   After many happy years dancing in the dance studio, at the numerous International Folklore Festivals in countries which have included the Ukraine, Romania, Bulgaria, Hungary, Poland, Germany and at venues all over the United Kingdom it is a great pleasure for me to record steps of the north-eastern region which have been passed down over many years.

Hopefully with the help of this book written for beginners through to intermediate level, dancers and traditional enthusiasts alike will enjoy the exhilaration and fun of clog dancing whilst learning steps and at the same time keep this art alive.

Happy clogging!

Robert Oley
2007

CONTENTS

Introduction

There are many different reasons for getting involved in this wonderful pastime and for whatever reason the pleasures of clog dancing can be enjoyed by anyone who has a will to learn. For those of you who wish to learn this book should prove invaluable but before I go any further I would like to write a little about the history of how this fine art began.

Clogs were worn by the working class people during the early 1800s in the industrial areas in the North of England. The hardwearing wood of the clog was ideal for working in the coal mines but also ideal for creating rhythms by tapping beats with the wooden soles. Steps were created and participants of this dance style became competitive. Competitions were arranged and many challenges took place to find a "champion" clog dancer. Music hall stages were also graced by these nimble footed virtuosos and celebrities such as Charlie Chaplin, Dan Leno and Stan Laurel, to mention only a few, were amongst them. Johnson Ellwood was a well-known clog dancer and music hall performer from the North-east and my collection of steps were taught to me by his daughter, Mary. The Ellwood family kept this tradition going for many years.

This unique form of percussive dancing was introduced to America towards the 19th century where upon it quickly developed into tap dancing. Clogs were replaced with split sole shoes which had wooden heels and progressed to dance shoes with metal taps on the toes and heels. The small music hall stage was now a theatre stage, much larger for the broader movement achieved by wearing tap shoes rather than clogs.

Clog dancers continue to clog dance but sometimes the steps are forgotten or changed. Hopefully having a list of these authentic steps noted in detail will keep these steps intact and prevent them from being lost altogether.

This is one good reason to get going and give it a try!

The style of Durham & Northumberland clog dancing

All the steps are performed on the balls of the feet which requires a certain amount of balance. The dropping of heels is a characteristic of this style and also the stance which requires the body to be held upright, as with the Irish dancer. The arms are kept at the sides of the body, relaxed, with no movement. The dance is called a hornpipe. Accompanying music should be a "dotted" hornpipe played on an accordion, fiddle, piano, whistle or similar instrument and should compliment the sound of the clog beats.

The content of a step

Each step consists of 16 bars. A "6 bar phrase" plus a "2 bar phrase" making 8 bars and repeated on the opposite side making 16 bars altogether. The "2 bar phrase" is 'a break'.

The sequences of the "6 bar phrases" are as follows :-

- 3 x "2 bar phrases" repeated, either on the same side or alternate sides;

- a "2 bar phrase" repeated on the opposite side plus a "2 bar variation";

- 6 x "1 bar phrases" repeated on the same side or alternate sides;

- or there are a few steps which do not fit into any of the above sequences and have obviously been designed to continue a good rhythm with a good movement in a different pattern

The final "2 bar phrase", 'the break', is always added to the "6 bar phrase" to complete a half step and enable a dancer to change from one side to the other. Breaks are listed in the index at beginners and intermediate levels.

A traditional hornpipe

The traditional hornpipe, which is danced as a solo dance at competitions, includes six full steps plus a step called a "double shuffle". A championship hornpipe includes ten full steps plus a "double shuffle". A good dance should include a variety of steps which have a good pattern of movement, good rhythms and be pleasing to the eye and ear. Any breaks can be added to any steps other than the last step, the "double shuffle", which has the "basic break". The speed of the dancing, the tempo, is determined by the ability and experience of the dancer. In competitions the musician determines the speed but otherwise whichever speed the dancer feels comfortable with, so as not to spoil their technique or the quality of the step, may be used. As a beginner 116 beats per minute is a good tempo to aim for. Most of the steps are to be executed "on the spot" but there are a few travelling steps which can be included to make the dance more interesting. Appropriate "on the spot" steps can also make a full turn.

Getting started

A wooden floor or wooden board and a pair of clogs, similar to the laced-up working type, are the main requirements but a pair of leather soled shoes can be used initially and any floor, with the exception of concrete. Nowadays a clog maker is a rare commodity but clogs can be found by the determined dancer.

How to use this book

- Check out the following "Explanation of rhythms" and try to get a clear understanding as it relates to the counting shown at the right hand side of the step notation. This will ensure you have the correct rhythm before attempting to learn a step.

- Refer to the Glossary of steps to clarify the terminology used. As your repertoire grows the ability to follow the notation should become easier.

- As most clog steps do not have names I have had to make the step titles relate to the content of the step and hopefully as you familiarise yourself with the steps, the title should give you an indication as to which step you are learning or checking out.

- The step categories, which are noted at the top corner of each page and listed in the index, have been categorized with the most prominent or difficult movement to indicate which category they have been listed in. You will notice many of the movements, for example "a toe to heel clip" may be entered into a different category where an alternative movement is dominating the step. E.g. The step "Toe to heel clip, **heel to toe clip** & stepping back" is listed under '**heel to toe clips**' as this is the most difficult movement in the step.

Explanation of rhythms

All the steps in this book are danced in 4/4 time which means the counting is in groups of 4. One group of 4 is one bar. These 4 counts can be made up of beats with different durational values to create rhythms and are shown broken down beside each dance movement to enable dancers to define the correct rhythm. When there is a pause in the rhythm, this is shown in my notation with brackets e.g. (-)

1 sound in one count is a crochet. These are whole counts and clapped evenly as follows :-
1 2 3 4

2 sounds in one count can be clapped even or uneven as follows :-
1& 2& 3& 4& (even) or 1(&)a 2(&)a 3(&)a 4(&)a (uneven). The even half counts are quavers and the uneven counts are triplets containing a pause.

3 sounds in one count are triplets, even and quick as follows :-
1&a 2&a 3&a 4&a

4 sounds in one count are semi-quavers, even and very quick as follows :-
1&&a 2&&a 3&&a 4&&a

Hearing the rhythms before attempting a step can be helpful. Try clapping the counts, allowing for the pauses in brackets.

Here are some examples to try :-

1& 2& 3&a 4   1   2&a 3 (4)   1&&a 2&a 3&a 4   1&a 2& 3 (4)

(accenting the whole counts can help)

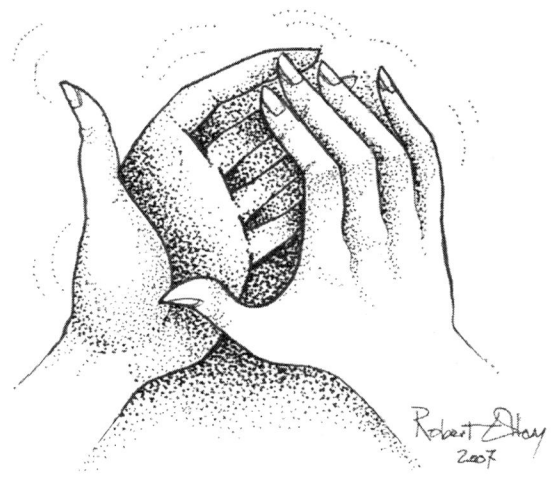

Index of Steps

Beginners

"Off the toe"

Dropping heels

Intermediate Steps

"Off the toe"

Dropping heels

Twizzles

Toe to heel clips

Toe to heel clips (continued)

Single & double jumps (continued)

No category

Breaks

Breaks (continued)

Robert Ashew
2007

First schottische

(repeats 6 times on alternate sides)

Step L	1
Shuffle R	&2
Step R-L	&3
Hop L (extending R foot in front in aerial position)	4

Step R	5
Shuffle L	&6
Step L-R	&7
Hop R (extending L foot in front in aerial position)	8

Step L	1
Shuffle R	&2
Step R-L	&3
Hop L (extending R foot in front in aerial position)	4

Step R	5
Shuffle L	&6
Step L-R	&7
Hop R (extending L foot in front in aerial position)	8

Continued/

1

"OFF THE
TOE"

/continued

Step L	1
Shuffle R	&2
Step R-L	&3
Hop L (extending R foot in front in aerial position)	4

Step R	5
Shuffle L	&6
Step L-R	&7
Hop R (extending L foot in front in aerial position)	8

Break - R   2 bars

Repeat all on opposite side   8 bars

BEGINNERS (vertical sidebar)

First schottische progression

(repeats 6 times on alternate sides)

Step L	1
Shuffle R	&2
Step R-L	&3
Hop L Shuffle R	4&a

Step R	5
Shuffle L	&6
Step L-R	&7
Hop R Shuffle L	8&a

Step L	1
Shuffle R	&2
Step R-L	&3
Hop L Shuffle R	4&a

Step R	5
Shuffle L	&6
Step L-R	&7
Hop R Shuffle L	8&a

Continued/

3

"OFF THE
    TOE"

/continued

Step L	1
Shuffle R	&2
Step R-L	&3
Hop L Shuffle R	4&a

Step R	5
Shuffle L	&6
Step L-R	&7
Hop R Shuffle L	8&a

Break - R	2 bars

Repeat all on opposite side	8 bars

4

B
E
G
I
N
N
E
R
S

Second schottische

(repeats 6 times on alternate sides)

Step L	1
Shuffle R	&2
Step R across L Step L in place	&3
Hop L (extending R foot in front in aerial position)	4

Step R	5
Shuffle L	&6
Step L across R Step R in place	&7
Hop R (extending L foot in front in aerial position)	8

Step L	1
Shuffle R	&2
Step R across L Step L in place	&3
Hop L (extending R foot in front in aerial position)	4

Step R	5
Shuffle L	&6
Step L across R Step R in place	&7
Hop R (extending L foot in front in aerial position)	8

Continued/

5

"OFF THE
TOE"

/continued

Step L	1
Shuffle R	&2
Step R across L Step L in place	&3
Hop L (extending R foot in front in aerial position)	4

Step R	5
Shuffle L	&6
Step L across R Step R in place	&7
Hop R (extending L foot in front in aerial position)	8

Break - R	2 bars

Repeat all on opposite side	8 bars

6

<u>Second schottische progression</u>

Step L	1
Shuffle R	&2
Step R across L Step L in place	&3
Hop L Shuffle R	4&a
Step R	5
Shuffle L	&6
Step L behind R Step R in place	&7
Hop R Shuffle L	8&a
Step L	1
Shuffle R	&2
Step R across L Step L in place	&3
Hop L Shuffle R	4&a
Step R	5
Shuffle L	&6
Step L behind R Step R in place	&7
Hop R Shuffle L	8&a

Continued/

7

"OFF THE
TOE"

/continued

Step L	1
Shuffle R	&2
Step R across L Step L in place	&3
Hop L Shuffle R	4&a

Step R	5
Shuffle L	&6
Step L behind R Step R in place	&7
Hop R Shuffle L	8&a

Break - R   2 bars

Repeat all on opposite side   8 bars

8

<u>Third schottische</u>

Step L	1
Shuffle R	&2
Step R-L	&3
Hop L (extending R foot in front in aerial position)	4
Step R	5
Shuffle L	&6
Step L-R	&7
Hop R (extending L foot in front in aerial position)	8
Step L to side	1
Step R across L Step L in place	(&)a2
Step R to side	3
Step L across R Step R in place	(&)a4
Step L	5
Shuffle R	&6
Step R-L	&7
Hop L (extending R foot in front in aerial position)	8

Continued/

"OFF THE
 TOE"

/continued

Step R to side	1
Step L across R Step R in place	(&)a2
Step L to side	3
Step R across L Step L in place	(&)a4
Step R	5
Shuffle L	&6
Step L-R	&7
Hop R (extending L foot in front in aerial position)	8

Break – R   2 bars

Repeat all on opposite side   8 bars

10

<u>Single & triple shuffles</u> (with variation)

Step L	1
Shuffle R Hop L	&a2
Step R	3
Shuffle L Hop R	&a4
Step L	5
Shuffle R Hop L	&a6
Shuffle R Hop L	&a7
Shuffle R Hop L	&a8
Step R	1
Shuffle L Hop R	&a2
Step L	3
Shuffle R Hop L	&a4
Step R	5
Shuffle L Hop R	&a6
Shuffle L Hop R	&a7
Shuffle L Hop R	&a8

Continued/

"OFF THE
TOE"

/continued

Variation –

Step L	1
Shuffle R Hop L	&a2
Shuffle R Hop L	&a3
Shuffle R Hop L	&a4
Step R	5
Shuffle L Hop R	&a6
Shuffle L Hop R	&a7
Shuffle L Hop R	&a8

Break – R   2 bars

Repeat all on opposite side   8 bars

<u>Double shuffle</u>

(repeats 12 times on alternate sides)

Step L
Shuffle R Hop L Shuffle R

1
&a2&a

Step R
Shuffle L Hop R Shuffle L

3
&a4&a

Step L
Shuffle R Hop L Shuffle R

5
&a6&a

Step R
Shuffle L Hop R Shuffle L

7
&a8&a

Step L
Shuffle R Hop L Shuffle R

1
&a2&a

Step R
Shuffle L Hop R Shuffle L

3
&a4&a

Step L
Shuffle R Hop L Shuffle R

5
&a6&a

Step R
Shuffle L Hop R Shuffle L

7
&a8&a

Continued/

13

"OFF THE
    TOE"

**B
E
G
I
N
N
E
R
S**

/continued

Step L	1
Shuffle R Hop L Shuffle R	&a2&a
Step R	3
Shuffle L Hop R Shuffle L	&a4&a
Step L	5
Shuffle R Hop L Shuffle R	&a6&a
Step R	7
Shuffle L Hop R Shuffle L	&a8&a
	2 bars
Break – R	
Repeat all on opposite side	8 bars

Stepping back (without heel beat)

(repeats 6 times on alternate sides)

Tap step L	&1
Shuffle R	&2
Hop L Step R behind L	&3
Tap Step L	&4
Tap step R	&5
Shuffle L	&6
Hop R Step L behind R	&7
Tap Step R	&8
Tap step L	&1
Shuffle R	&2
Hop L Step R behind L	&3
Tap Step L	&4
Tap step R	&5
Shuffle L	&6
Hop R Step L behind R	&7
Tap Step R	&8

Continued/

15

"OFF THE
    TOE"

/continued

Tap step L	&1
Shuffle R	&2
Hop L Step R behind L	&3
Tap Step L	&4
Tap step R	&5
Shuffle L	&6
Hop R Step L behind R	&7
Tap Step R	&8

Break – R   2 bars

Repeat all on opposite side   8 bars

16

<u>Stepping over</u>

(repeats 6 times on same side)

Tap step L	&1
Shuffle R	&2
Ball dig R across (with weight) Heel beat R	&a
Step L	3
Tap step R in place	&4

Tap step L	&5
Shuffle R	&6
Ball dig R across (with weight) Heel beat R	&a
Step L	7
Tap step R in place	&8

Tap step L	&1
Shuffle R	&2
Ball dig R across (with weight) Heel beat R	&a
Step L	3
Tap step R in place	&4

Tap step L	&5
Shuffle R	&6
Ball dig R across (with weight) Heel beat R	&a
Step L	7
Tap step R in place	&8

Continued/

17

DROPPING
  HEELS

/continued

Tap step L	&1
Shuffle R	&2
Ball dig R across (with weight) Heel beat R	&a
Step L	3
Tap step R in place	&4
Tap step L	&5
Shuffle R	&6
Ball dig R across (with weight) Heel beat R	&a
Step L	7
Tap step R in place	&8

Break – R   2 bars

Repeat all on opposite side   8 bars

<u>Stepping back</u>

(repeats 6 times on alternate side)

Tap step L	&1
Shuffle R	&2
Hop L Heel beat L Step R behind L	&a3
Tap step L	&4

Tap step R	&5
Shuffle L	&6
Hop R Heel beat R Step L behind R	&a7
Tap step R	&8

Tap step L	&1
Shuffle R	&2
Hop L Heel beat L Step R behind L	&a3
Tap step L	&4

Tap step R	&5
Shuffle L	&6
Hop R Heel beat R Step L behind R	&a7
Tap step R	&8

Continued/

B
E
G
I
N
N
E
R
S

DROPPING
HEELS

/continued

Tap step L	&1
Shuffle R	&2
Hop L Heel beat L Step R behind L	&a3
Tap step L	&4

Tap step R	&5
Shuffle L	&6
Hop R Heel beat R Step L behind R	&a7
Tap step R	&8

Break – R   2 bars

Repeat all on opposite side   8 bars

20

<u>Stepping over & stepping back</u>

Tap step L	&1
Shuffle R	&2
Ball dig R across (with weight) Heel beat R	&a
Step L in place	3
Tap step R by side of L	&4
Tap step L	&5
Shuffle R	&6
Ball dig R across (with weight) Heel beat R	&a
Step L in place	7
Tap step R by side of L	&8
Tap step L	&1
Shuffle R	&2
Hop L Heel beat L Step R behind L	&a3
Tap Step L	&4
Tap step R	&5
Shuffle L	&6
Hop R Heel beat R Step L behind R	&a7
Tap Step R	&8

Continued/

21

DROPPING
HEELS

/continued

Tap step L	&1
Shuffle R	&2
Ball dig R across (with weight) Heel beat R	&a
Step L in place	3
Tap step R by side of L	&4
Tap step L	&5
Shuffle R	&6
Ball dig R across (with weight) Heel beat R	&a
Step L in place	7
Tap step R by side of L	&8

Break – R   2 bars

Repeat all on opposite side   8 bars

22

Stepping over & stepping back alternative

Tap step L	&1
Shuffle R	&2
Ball dig R across (with weight) Heel beat R	&a
Step L in place	3
Tap step R by side of L	&4
Tap step L	&5
Shuffle R	&6
Hop L Heel beat L Step R behind L	&a7
Tap Step L	&8
Tap step R	&1
Shuffle L	&2
Ball dig L across (with weight) Heel beat L	&a
Step R in place	3
Tap step L by side of R	&4
Tap step R	&5
Shuffle L	&6
Hop R Heel beat R Step L behind R	&a7
Tap Step R	&8

Continued/

23

DROPPING
HEELS

/continued

Tap step L	&1
Shuffle R	&2
Ball dig R across (with weight) Heel beat R	&a
Step L in place	3
Tap step R by side of L	&4
Tap step L	&5
Shuffle R	&6
Hop L Heel beat L Step R behind L	&a7
Tap Step L	&8

Break – R commencing with 'Hop L' instead of
'Step L' to continue break on the correct side   2 bars

Repeat all on opposite side   8 bars

**B
E
G
I
N
N
E
R
S**

<u>Single twizzles</u> (with variation)

Step L	1
Shuffle R twice (4 beat Single twizzle)	(&)a2&a
Step R	3
Shuffle L twice (4 beat Single twizzle)	(&)a4&a
Step L	5
Shuffle Step R	&a6
Shuffle Step L	&a7
Shuffle R twice (4 beat Single twizzle)	(&)a8&a
Step R	1
Shuffle L twice (4 beat Single twizzle)	(&)a2&a
Step L	3
Shuffle R twice (4 beat Single twizzle)	(&)a4&a
Step R	5
Shuffle Step L	&a6
Shuffle Step R	&a7
Shuffle L twice (4 beat Single twizzle)	(&)a8&a

Continued/

25

/continued

Variation –

Step L	1
Shuffle Step R	&a2
Shuffle Step L	&a3
Shuffle R twice (4 beat Single twizzle)	(&)a4&a
Step R	5
Shuffle Step L	&a6
Shuffle Step R	&a7
Shuffle L twice (4 beat Single twizzle)	(&)a8&a

Break – R   2 bars

Repeat all on opposite side   8 bars

<u>Single twizzles alternative</u> (with variation)

Step L	1
Shuffle R twice (4 beat Single twizzle)	(&)a2&a
Step R	3
Shuffle L twice (4 beat Single twizzle)	(&)a4&a
Step L	5
Shuffle R twice (4 beat Single twizzle)	(&)a6&a
Step R Shuffle L	7&a
Step L Shuffle R	8&a

Step R	1
Shuffle L twice (4 beat Single twizzle)	(&)a2&a
Step L	3
Shuffle R twice (4 beat Single twizzle)	(&)a4&a
Step R	5
Shuffle L twice (4 beat Single twizzle)	(&)a6&a
Step L Shuffle R	7&a
Step R Shuffle L	8&a

Continued/

27

/continued

<u>Variation</u> –

Step L	1
Shuffle R twice (4 beat Single twizzle)	(&)a2&a
Step R	3
Shuffle Step L	&a4
Shuffle R	&a
Step R	5
Shuffle L twice (4 beat Single twizzle)	(&)a6&a
Step L	7
Shuffle Step R	&a8
Shuffle L	&a
Break – R	2 bars
Repeat all on opposite side	8 bars

Single twizzles & stepping back

Step L	1
Shuffle R twice (4 beat Single twizzle)	(&)a2&a
Step R	3
Shuffle L twice (4 beat Single twizzle)	(&)a4&a
Step L	5
Shuffle R	&6
Hop L Step R behind L	&7
Tap Step L	&8

Step R	1
Shuffle L twice (4 beat Single twizzle)	(&)a2&a
Step L	3
Shuffle R twice (4 beat Single twizzle)	(&)a4&a
Step R	5
Shuffle L	&6
Hop R Step L behind R	&7
Tap Step R	&8

Continued/

29

/continued

Step L	1
Shuffle R twice (4 beat Single twizzle)	(&)a2&a
Step R	3
Shuffle L twice (4 beat Single twizzle)	(&)a4&a
Step L	5
Shuffle R	&6
Hop L Step R behind L	&7
Tap Step L	&8

Break - R commencing with 'Hop L' instead of
'Step L' to continue break on the correct side   2 bars

Repeat all on opposite side   8 bars

B E G I N N E R S

<u>Single twizzles & stepping back</u> (with variation)

Step L	1
Shuffle R twice (4 beat Single twizzle)	(&)a2&a
Step R	3
Shuffle L twice (4 beat Single twizzle)	(&)a4&a
Step L	5
Shuffle R	&6
Hop L Step R behind L	&7
Tap Step L	&8

Step R	1
Shuffle L twice (4 beat Single twizzle)	(&)a2&a
Step L	3
Shuffle R twice (4 beat Single twizzle)	(&)a4&a
Step R	5
Shuffle L	&6
Hop R Step L behind R	&7
Tap Step R	&8

Continued/

31

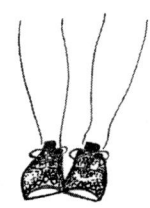

TWIZZLES

/continued

<u>Variation</u> –

Step L	1
Shuffle R	&2
Hop L Step R behind L	&3
Tap Step L	&4
Step R	5
Shuffle L	&6
Hop R Step L behind R	&7
Tap Step R	&8

Break – R   2 bars

Repeat all on opposite side   8 bars

Single heels & single jump (with variation)

Step L	1
Heel dig R Step L	(&)a2
Step R	3
Heel dig L Step R	(&)a4
Step L	5
Heel dig R Step L	(&)a6
Ball dig R (with weight) Step L	(&)a7
Spring onto both feet with R foot in front of L	8

Step R	1
Heel dig L Step R	(&)a2
Step L	3
Heel dig R Step L	(&)a4
Step R	5
Heel dig L Step R	(&)a6
Ball dig L (with weight) Step R	(&)a7
Spring onto both feet with L foot in front of R	8

Continued/

33

SINGLE
JUMPS

/continued

Variation –

Step L	1
Heel dig R Step L	(&)a2
Ball dig R (with weight) Step L	(&)a3
Spring onto both feet with R foot in front of L	4
Step R	5
Heel dig L Step R	(&)a6
Ball dig L (with weight) Step R	(&)a7
Spring onto both feet with L foot in front of R	8

Break – R   2 bars

Repeat all on opposite side   8 bars

<u>Single and double heels</u> (with variation)

Step L	1
Heel dig R Step L	(&)a2
Step R	3
Heel dig L Step R	(&)a4
Step L	5
Heel dig R Step L	(&)a6
Ball dig R (with weight) Step L	(&)a7
Heel dig R Step L	(&)a8
Step R	1
Heel dig L Step R	(&)a2
Step L	3
Heel dig R Step L	(&)a4
Step R	5
Heel dig L Step R	(&)a6
Ball dig L (with weight) Step R	(&)a7
Heel dig L Step R	(&)a8

Continued/

/continued

<u>Variation</u> -

Step L	1
Heel dig R Step L	(&)a2
Ball dig R (with weight) Step L	(&)a3
Heel dig R Step L	(&)a4
Step R	5
Heel dig L Step R	(&)a6
Ball dig L (with weight) Step R	(&)a7
Heel dig L Step R	(&)a8

Break – R | 2 bars

Repeat all on opposite side | 8 bars

<u>Umpas</u> (with variation)

Spring L behind (extending R foot forward in
aerial position)   1
Spring R in place   2
Spring L behind (extending R foot forward in
aerial position)   3
Spring R in place   4

Step L in place   5
Shuffle R   &6
Hop L Toe tap R behind   &7
Slap R   8

Spring R behind (extending L foot forward in
aerial position)   1
Spring L in place   2
Spring R behind (extending L foot forward in
aerial position)   3
Spring L in place   4

Step R in place   5
Shuffle L   &6
Hop R Toe tap L behind   &7
Slap L   8

Continued/

37

**B
E
G
I
N
N
E
R
S**

/continued

<u>Variation</u> –

Step L in place	1
Shuffle R	&2
Hop L Toe tap R behind	&3
Slap R	4
Step R in place	5
Shuffle L	&6
Hop R Toe tap L behind	&7
Slap L	8

Break – R   2 bars

Repeat all on the opposite side   8 bars

Basic

(a) "Off the toe"

R side –

Step L	1
Shuffle R	&2
Step R-L	&3
Shuffle R	&4
Spring R Straight tap L in front	&5
Step L in place	6
Ball dig R across L	7
Pause	(8)

L side –

Step R	1
Shuffle L	&2
Step L-R	&3
Shuffle L	&4
Spring L Straight tap R in front	&5
Step R in place	6
Ball dig L across R	7
Pause	(8)

Basic

(b) Dropping heels

R side –

Step L	1
Shuffle R	&2
Ball dig R (with weight) Heel beat R Step L	&a3
Shuffle R	&4
Ball dig R (with weight) Heel beat R	&a
Straight tap L in front	5
Step L in place	6
Ball dig R across L	7
Pause	(8)

L side –

Step R	1
Shuffle L	&2
Ball dig L (with weight) Heel beat L Step R	&a3
Shuffle L	&4
Ball dig L (with weight) Heel beat L	&a
Straight tap R in front	5
Step R in place	6
Ball dig L across R	7
Pause	(8)

Twizzle slap

R side –

Step L	1
Shuffle R twice (4 beat Single twizzle)	(&)a2&a
Step R	3
Shuffle L twice (4 beat Single twizzle)	(&)a4&a
Step L	5
Shuffle Step R	&a6
Shuffle Step L	&a7
Slap R	8

L side –

Step R	1
Shuffle L twice (4 beat Single twizzle)	(&)a2&a
Step L	3
Shuffle R twice (4 beat Single twizzle)	(&)a4&a
Step R	5
Shuffle Step L	&a6
Shuffle Step R	&a7
Slap L	8

41

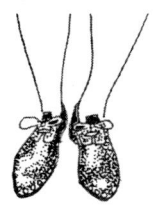

"OFF THE
    TOE"

Single and double trebles (with variation)

<table>
<tr>
<td>Spring L Shuffle R
Step R-L
Shuffle R</td>
<td>}</td>
<td>Single treble R</td>
<td>1&&
a2
&a</td>
</tr>
<tr>
<td>Spring R Shuffle L
Step L-R
Shuffle L</td>
<td>}</td>
<td>Single treble L</td>
<td>3&&
a4
&a</td>
</tr>
<tr>
<td>Spring L Shuffle R
Step R-L
Shuffle R
Hop L Shuffle R
Step R-L
Shuffle R</td>
<td>}</td>
<td>Double treble R</td>
<td>5&&
a6
&a
7&&
a8
&a</td>
</tr>
<tr>
<td>Spring R Shuffle L
Step L-R
Shuffle L</td>
<td>}</td>
<td>Single treble L</td>
<td>1&&
a2
&a</td>
</tr>
<tr>
<td>Spring L Shuffle R
Step R-L
Shuffle R</td>
<td>}</td>
<td>Single treble R</td>
<td>3&&
a4
&a</td>
</tr>
</table>

I N T E R M E D I A T E

Continued/

/continued

Spring R Shuffle L	⎫	5&&
Step L-R		a6
Shuffle L	Double treble L	&a
Hop R Shuffle L		7&&
Step L-R		a8
Shuffle L	⎭	&a

Variation –

Spring L Shuffle R	⎫	1&&
Step R-L		a2
Shuffle R	Double treble R	&a
Hop L Shuffle R		3&&
Step R-L		a4
Shuffle R	⎭	&a

Spring R Shuffle L	⎫	5&&
Step L-R		a6
Shuffle L	Double treble L	&a
Hop R Shuffle L		7&&
Step L-R		a8
Shuffle L	⎭	&a

Break – R   2 bars

INTERMEDIATE

Repeat all on opposite side   8 bars

43

Shuffles & elevated side clip (heel to heel)

Step L	1
Shuffle R Step R	&a2
Shuffle L Step L	&a3
Raise R leg to R side –	(&)
Hop L & clip R heel with L heel (inside of heels	a4
touching)	
Hop L	5
Shuffle R Step R	&a6
Shuffle L Step L	&a7
Shuffle R Hop L	&a8
Step R	1
Shuffle L Step L	&a2
Shuffle R Step R	&a3
Raise L leg to L side –	(&)
Hop R & clip L heel with R heel (inside of heels	a4
touching)	
Hop R	5
Shuffle L Step L	&a6
Shuffle R Step R	&a7
Shuffle R Hop R	&a8

I
N
T
E
R
M
E
D
I
A
T
E

Continued/

/continued

Step L	1
Shuffle R Step R	&a2
Shuffle L Step L	&a3
Raise R leg to R side -	(&)
Hop L & clip R heel with L heel (inside of heels touching)	a4
Hop L	5
Shuffle R Step R	&a6
Shuffle L Step L	&a7
Shuffle R Hop L	&a8

Break – R commencing with 'Hop L' instead of 'Step L' to continue break on the correct side   2 bars

Repeat all on opposite side   8 bars

INTERMEDIATE

45

DROPPING
  HEELS

Stepping over & clip toes & heels together

Tap step L	&1
Shuffle R	&2
Ball dig R across (with weight) Heel beat R	&a
Step L in place	3
Tap step R by side of L	&4
Heel dig L-R	&5
Clip toes together	&
Step L-R	a6
Clip heels together	&
Spring L	a
Shuffle R	7&
Hop L Ball dig R	a8
Tap step R	&1
Shuffle L	&2
Ball dig L across (with weight) Heel beat L	&a
Step R in place	3
Tap step L by side of R	&4
Heel dig R-L	&5
Clip toes together	&
Step R-L	a6
Clip heels together	&
Spring R	a
Shuffle L	7&
Hop R Ball dig L	a8

Continued/

INTERMEDIATE

/continued

Tap step L	&1
Shuffle R	&2
Ball dig R across (with weight) Heel beat R	&a
Step L in place	3
Tap step R by side of L	&4
Heel dig L-R	&5
Clip toes together	&
Step L-R	a6
Clip heels together	&
Spring L	a
Shuffle R	7&
Hop L Ball dig R (with weight)	a8
Break – R	2 bars
Repeat all on opposite side	8 bars

INTERMEDIATE

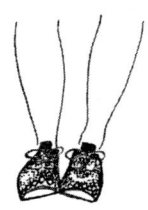

DROPPING
  HEELS

Stepping over & clip toes & heels together
(with variation)

Tap step L	&1
Shuffle R	&2
Ball dig R across (with weight) Heel beat R	&a
Step L in place	3
Tap step R by side of L	&4
Heel dig L-R	&5
Clip toes together	&
Step L-R	a6
Clip heels together	&
Spring L	a
Shuffle R	7&
Hop L Ball dig R	a8
Tap step R	&1
Shuffle L	&2
Ball dig L across (with weight) Heel beat L	&a
Step R in place	3
Tap step L by side of R	&4
Heel dig R-L	&5
Clip toes together	&
Step R-L	a6
Clip heels together	&
Spring R	a
Shuffle L	7&
Hop R Ball dig L	a8

Continued/

(left margin, vertical text) INTERMEDIATE

/continued

Variation –

Heel dig L-R	&1
Clip toes together	&
Step L-R	a2
Clip heels together	&
Spring L	a
Shuffle R	3&
Hop L Ball dig R	a4

Heel dig R-L	&5
Clip toes together	&
Step R-L	a6
Clip heels together	&
Spring R	a
Shuffle L	7&
Hop R Ball dig L	a8

Break – R   2 bars

Repeat all on opposite side   8 bars

INTERMEDIATE

49

DROPPING
  HEELS

Ball heel & over & hop (with variation)

Step L	1
Ball dig R in front (with weight) Heel beat R	&a
Step L	2
Step R	3
Ball dig L in front (with weight) Heel beat L	&a
Step R	4
Step L	5
Shuffle R Hop L	&a6
Ball dig R across L (with weight) Heel beat R	&a
Step L in place	7
Ball dig R in place (with weight) Heel beat R	&a
Ball dig L (with weight)	8
Step R	1
Ball dig L in front (with weight) Heel beat L	&a
Step R	2
Step L	3
Ball dig R in front (with weight) Heel beat R	&a
Step L	4
Step R	5
Shuffle L Hop R	&a6
Ball dig L across R (with weight) Heel beat L	&a
Step R in place	7
Ball dig L in place (with weight) Heel beat L	&a
Ball dig R (with weight)	8

Continued/

/continued

<u>Variation</u> -

Step L	1
Shuffle R Hop L	&a2
Ball dig R across L (with weight) Heel beat R	&a
Step L in place	3
Ball dig R in place (with weight) Heel beat R	&a
Ball dig L (with weight)	4
Step R	5
Shuffle L Hop R	&a6
Ball dig L across R (with weight) Heel beat L	&a
Step R in place	7
Ball dig L in place (with weight) Heel beat L	&a
Ball dig R (with weight)	8
Break – R	2 bars
Repeat all on opposite side	8 bars

I N T E R M E D I A T E

51

DROPPING
   HEELS

Shuffle across & ball heel step (with variation)

Tap step L	&1
Shuffle R Heel beat L (turning R knee out, bring R heel across L)	&a2
Tap step R	&3
Shuffle L Heel beat R (turning L knee out, bring L heel across R)	&a4
Tap step L	&5
Tap step R	&6
Tap step L	&7
Ball dig R in front (with weight) Heel beat R	&a
Step L in place	8
Tap step R	&1
Shuffle L Heel beat R (turning L knee out, bring L heel across R)	&a2
Tap step L	&3
Shuffle R Heel beat L (turning R knee out, bring R heel across L)	&a4
Tap step R	&5
Tap step L	&6
Tap step R	&7
Ball dig L in front (with weight) Heel beat L	&a
Step R in place	8

Continued/

(Vertical text in left margin: INTERMEDIATE)

/continued

Variation –

Tap step L	&1
Tap step R	&2
Tap step L	&3
Ball dig R in front (with weight) Heel beat R	&a
Step L in place	4
Tap step R	&5
Tap step L	&6
Tap step R	&7
Ball dig L in front (with weight) Heel beat L	&a
Step R in place	8
Break – R	2 bars
Repeat all on opposite side	8 bars

INTERMEDIATE

53

<u>Irish rover</u> (with variation)

Step L	1
Shuffle R Hop L Shuffle R	&a2&a
Step R	3
Shuffle L Hop R Shuffle L	&a4&a
Step L	5
Shuffle R Hop L	&a6
Ball dig R across L (with weight) Heel beat R	&a
Step L in place	7
Ball dig R in place (with weight) Heel beat R	&a
Step L in place	8
Step R	1
Shuffle L Hop R Shuffle L	&a2&a
Step L	3
Shuffle R Hop L Shuffle R	&a4&a
Step R	5
Shuffle L Hop R	&a6
Ball dig L across R (with weight) Heel beat L	&a
Step R in place	7
Ball dig L in place (with weight) Heel beat L	&a
Step R in place	8

Continued/

(Side margin, vertical text: INTERMEDIATE)

/continued

Variation –

Step L	1
Shuffle R Hop L	&a2
Ball dig R across L (with weight) Heel beat R	&a
Step L in place	3
Ball dig R in place (with weight) Heel beat R	&a
Step L in place	4
Step R	5
Shuffle L Hop R	&a6
Ball dig L across L (with weight) Heel beat L	&a
Step R in place	7
Ball dig L in place (with weight) Heel beat L	&a
Step R in place	8

Break – R   2 bars

Repeat all on opposite side   8 bars

I
N
T
E
R
M
E
D
I
A
T
E

55

DROPPING
HEELS

First military

(repeats 6 times on alternate sides)

INTERMEDIATE

Tap step L	&1
Shuffle R	&2
Ball dig R (with weight) Heel beat R	&3
Shuffle L Ball dig L (with weight) Heel beat L	&&a4
Tap step R	&5
Shuffle L	&6
Ball dig L (with weight) Heel beat L	&7
Shuffle R Ball dig R (with weight) Heel beat R	&&a8
Tap step L	&1
Shuffle R	&2
Ball dig R (with weight) Heel beat R	&3
Shuffle L Ball dig L (with weight) Heel beat L	&&a4
Tap step R	&5
Shuffle L	&6
Ball dig L (with weight) Heel beat L	&7
Shuffle R Ball dig R (with weight) Heel beat R	&&a8

Continued/

/continued

Tap step L	&1
Shuffle R	&2
Ball dig R (with weight) Heel beat R	&3
Shuffle L Ball dig L (with weight) Heel beat L	&&a4
Tap step R	&5
Shuffle L	&6
Ball dig L (with weight) Heel beat L	&7
Shuffle R Ball dig R (with weight) Heel beat R	&&a8
Break – R	2 bars
Repeat all on opposite side	8 bars

INTERMEDIATE

57

DROPPING
  HEELS

Second military (with variation)

Tap step L	&1
Shuffle R Heel beat L (turning R knee out)	&a2
Tap step R	&3
Brush L forward Heel beat R	&4
Brush L backward Step L	&5
Shuffle R	&6
Ball dig R (with weight) Heel beat R	&7
Shuffle L Ball dig L (with weight) Heel beat L	&&a8
Tap step R	&1
Shuffle L Heel beat R (turning R knee out)	&a2
Tap step L	&3
Brush R forward Heel beat L	&4
Brush R backward Step R	&5
Shuffle L	&6
Ball dig L (with weight) Heel beat L	&7
Shuffle R Ball dig R (with weight) Heel beat R	&&a8

Continued/

(vertical sidebar text) INTERMEDIATE

/continued

Variation –

Tap step L	&1
Shuffle R Heel beat L (turning R knee out)	&a2
Tap step R	&3
Brush L forward Heel beat R	&4
Brush L backward Step L	&5
Shuffle R Heel beat L (turning R knee cut)	&a6
Tap step R	&7
Brush L forward Heel beat R	&8

Break – R   2 bars

Repeat all on opposite side   8 bars

INTERMEDIATE

DROPPING
HEELS

Stamp & shuffles (with variation)

Step L		1
Straight tap R		2
Shuffle R	Stamp R	&3
Ball dig R (with weight) Heel beat R		&a
Ball dig L		4

	&5
Ball dig L (with weight) Heel beat L	&&a6
Shuffle R Ball dig R (with weight) Heel beat R	&&a7
Shuffle L Ball dig L (with weight) Heel beat L	8
Slap R	

Step R		1
Straight tap L		2
Shuffle L	Stamp L	&3
Ball dig L (with weight) Heel beat L		&a
Ball dig R		4

Ball dig R (with weight) Heel beat R	&5
Shuffle L Ball dig L (with weight) Heel beat L	&&a6
Shuffle R Ball dig R (with weight) Heel beat R	&&a7
Slap L	8

Continued/

60

INTERMEDIATE

/continued

Variation –

Ball dig L (with weight) Heel beat L	&1
Shuffle R Ball dig R (with weight) Heel beat R	&&a2
Shuffle L Ball dig L (with weight) Heel beat L	&&a3
Slap R	4
Ball dig R (with weight) Heel beat R	&5
Shuffle L Ball dig L (with weight) Heel beat L	&&a6
Shuffle R Ball dig R (with weight) Heel beat R	&&a7
Slap L	8
Break - R	2 bars
Repeat all on opposite side	8 bars

INTERMEDIATE

61

DROPPING
HEELS

Happy wanderer (with variation)

Step L	1
Forward tap R Heel beat L	&2
Shuffle R Ball dig R (with weight) Heel beat R	&&a3
Forward tap L Heel beat R	&4
Shuffle L Ball dig L (with weight) Heel beat L	&&a5
Shuffle R Ball dig R (with weight) Heel beat R	&&a6
Shuffle L Ball dig L (with weight) Heel beat L	&&a7
Forward tap R Heel beat L	&8
Shuffle R Ball dig R (with weight) Heel beat R	&&a1
Forward tap L Heel beat R	&2
Shuffle L Ball dig L (with weight) Heel beat L	&&a3
Forward tap R Heel beat L	&4
Shuffle R Ball dig R (with weight) Heel beat R	&&a5
Shuffle L Ball dig L (with weight) Heel beat L	&&a6
Shuffle R Ball dig R (with weight) Heel beat R	&&a7
Forward tap L Heel beat R	&8

Continued/

I N T E R M E D I A T E

/continued

Variation –

Shuffle L Ball dig L (with weight) Heel beat L	&&a1
Shuffle R Ball dig R (with weight) Heel beat R	&&a2
Shuffle L Ball dig L (with weight) Heel beat L	&&a3
Forward tap R Heel beat L	&4
Shuffle R Ball dig R (with weight) Heel beat R	&&a5
Shuffle L Ball dig L (with weight) Heel beat L	&&a6
Shuffle R Ball dig R (with weight) Heel beat R	&&a7
Forward tap L Heel beat R	&8
Break – R	2 bars
Repeat all on opposite side	8 bars

INTERMEDIATE

63

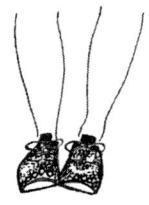

Over & hop & single heel

(Repeats 6 times on same side)

Step L	1
Shuffle R Hop L	&a2
Ball dig R across L (with weight) Heel beat R	&a
Step L in place	3
Ball dig R in place (with weight) Heel beat R	&a
Heel dig L	4
Ball dig R (with weight) Heel beat R	&a
Step L	5
Shuffle R Hop L	&a6
Ball dig R across L (with weight) Heel beat R	&a
Step L in place	7
Ball dig R in place (with weight) Heel beat R	&a
Heel dig L	8
Ball dig R (with weight) Heel beat R	&a
Step L	1
Shuffle R Hop L	&a2
Ball dig R across L (with weight) Heel beat R	&a
Step L in place	3
Ball dig R in place (with weight) Heel beat R	&a
Heel dig L	4
Ball dig R (with weight) Heel beat R	&a

Continued/

I
N
T
E
R
M
E
D
I
A
T
E

/continued

Step L	5
Shuffle R Hop L	&a6
Ball dig R across L (with weight) Heel beat R	&a
Step L in place	7
Ball dig R in place (with weight) Heel beat R	&a
Heel dig L	8
Ball dig R (with weight) Heel beat R	&a
Step L	1
Shuffle R Hop L	&a2
Ball dig R across L (with weight) Heel beat R	&a
Step L in place	3
Ball dig R in place (with weight) Heel beat R	&a
Heel dig L	4
Ball dig R (with weight) Heel beat R	&a
Step L	5
Shuffle R Hop L	&a6
Ball dig R across L (with weight) Heel beat R	&a
Step L in place	7
Ball dig R in place (with weight) Heel beat R	&a
Heel dig L	8
Ball dig R (with weight) Heel beat R	&a
Break – R	2 bars
Repeat all on opposite side	8 bars

INTERMEDIATE

65

<u>Over & hop & single heel progression</u>

Step L	1
Shuffle R Hop L	&a2
Ball dig R across L (with weight) Heel beat R	&a
Step L in place	3
Ball dig R in place (with weight) Heel beat R	&a
Heel dig L	4
Ball dig R (with weight) Heel beat R	&a
Step L	5
Shuffle R Hop L	&a6
Ball dig R across L (with weight) Heel beat R	&a
Step L in place	7
Ball dig R in place (with weight) Heel beat R	&a
Heel dig L	8
Ball dig R (with weight) Heel beat R	&a
Step L	1
Shuffle R Hop L	&a2
Ball dig R across L (with weight) Heel beat R	&a
Step L in place	3
Ball dig R in place (with weight) Heel beat R	&a
Heel dig L	4
Ball dig R (with weight) Heel beat R	&a

INTERMEDIATE

Continued/

/continued

Ball dig L (with weight)	5
Ball dig R in place (with weight) Heel beat R	&a
Heel dig L	6
Ball dig R (with weight) Heel beat R	&a
Ball dig L (with weight)	7
Ball dig R in place (with weight) Heel beat R	&a
Heel dig L	8
Ball dig R in place (with weight) Heel beat R	&a
Step L	1
Shuffle R Hop L	&a2
Ball dig R across L (with weight) Heel beat R	&a
Step L in place	3
Ball dig R in place (with weight) Heel beat R	&a
Heel dig L	4
Ball dig R (with weight) Heel beat R	&a
Step L	5
Shuffle R Hop L	&a6
Ball dig R across L (with weight) Heel beat R	&a
Step L in place	7
Ball dig R in place (with weight) Heel beat R	&a
Heel dig L	8
Ball dig R (with weight) Heel beat R	&a
Break – R	2 bars
Repeat all on opposite side	8 bars

INTERMEDIATE

Stamp & twizzle slap (with variation)

Step L		1
Straight tap R		2
Shuffle R	Stamp R	&3
Ball dig R (with weight) Heel beat R		&a
Ball dig L		4

Step L	5
Shuffle R twice (4 beat Single twizzle R)	(&)a6&a
Brush forward R	7
Slap R	8

Step R		1
Straight tap L		2
Shuffle L	Stamp L	&3
Ball dig L (with weight) Heel beat L		&a
Ball dig R		4

Step R	5
Shuffle L twice (4 beat Single twizzle L)	(&)a6&a
Brush forward L	7
Slap L	8

I N T E R M E D I A T E

Continued/

/continued

<u>Variation</u> –

Step L	1
Shuffle R twice (4 beat Single twizzle R)	(&)a2&a
Brush forward R	3
Slap R	4
Step R	5
Shuffle L twice (4 beat Single twizzle L)	(&)a6&a
Brush forward L	7
Slap L	8
Break – R	2 bars
Repeat all on opposite side	8 bars

I
N
T
E
R
M
E
D
I
A
T
E

Single & double twizzles (with variation)

Step L	1
Shuffle R twice (4 beat Single twizzle)	(&)a2&a
Step R	3
Shuffle L twice (4 beat Single twizzle)	(&)a4&a
Step L	5
Shuffle R 5 times (Double twizzle)	(&)a6&a7
	&a8&a
Step R	1
Shuffle L twice (4 beat Single twizzle)	(&)a2&a
Step L	3
Shuffle R twice (4 beat Single twizzle)	(&)a4&a
Step R	5
Shuffle L 5 times (Double twizzle)	(&)a6&a7
	&a8&a

INTERMEDIATE

Continued/

70

/continued

Variation –

Step L	1
Shuffle R 5 times (Double twizzle)	(&)a2&a3 &a4&a
Step R	5
Shuffle L 5 times (Double twizzle)	(&)a6&a7 &a8&a
Break – R	2 bars
Repeat all on opposite side	8 bars

INTERMEDIATE

71

<u>Twizzle stop</u> (with variation)

Step L	1
Shuffle R twice (4 beat Single twizzle)	(&)a2&a
Ball dig R	3
Shuffle R twice (4 beat Single twizzle)	(&)a4&a
Ball dig R	5
Shuffle R 5 times (Double twizzle)	(&)a6&a7
	&a8&a
	1
Step R	(&)a2&a
Shuffle L twice (4 beat Single twizzle)	3
Ball dig L	(&)a4&a
Shuffle L twice (4 beat Single twizzle)	
Ball dig L	5
Shuffle L 5 times (Double twizzle)	(&)a6&a7
	&a8&a

Continued/

I
N
T
E
R
M
E
D
I
A
T
E

/continued

Variation –

Step L	1
Shuffle R 5 times (Double twizzle)	(&)a2&a3 &a4&a
Step R	5
Shuffle L 5 times (Double twizzle)	(&)a6&a7 &a8&a
Break - R	2 bars
Repeat all on opposite side	8 bars

I N T E R M E D I A T E

73

TWIZZLES

Single jump, clip toes & heels together & twizzle slap

Spring onto the balls of both feet with R foot in front of L	1
Toe clip L to R heel (using outside of L toe to outside of R heel)	&
Heel beat R	2
Heel dig L-R	&3
Clip toes together	&
Step L-R	a4
Clip heels together	&
Step L	5
Shuffle R twice (4 beat Single twizzle)	(&)a6&a
Brush forward R	7
Slap R	8
Spring onto the balls of both feet with L foot in front of R	1
Toe clip R to L heel (using outside of R toe to outside of L heel)	&
Heel beat L	2
Heel dig R-L	&3
Clip toes together	&
Step R-L	a4
Clip heels together	&
Step R	5
Shuffle L twice (4 beat single twizzle)	(&)a6&a
Brush forward L	7
Slap L	8

Continued/

I N T E R M E D I A T E

/continued

Spring onto the balls of both feet with R foot in front of L	1
Toe clip L to R heel (using outside of L toe to outside of R heel)	&
Heel beat R	2
Heel dig L-R	&3
Clip toes together	&
Step L-R	a4
Clip heels together	&
Step L	5
Shuffle R twice (4 beat Single twizzle)	(&)a6&a
Brush forward R	7
Slap R	8

Break – R commencing with 'Hop L' instead of 'Step L' to continue break on the correct side .... 2 bars

Repeat all on opposite side .... 8 bars

INTERMEDIATE

Single jump, single twizzle & over & hop
(with variation)

Spring onto the balls of both feet with R foot in front of L	1
Toe clip L to R heel (using outside of L toe to outside of R heel)	&
Heel beat R	2
Step L	3
Shuffle R 3 times (6 beat Single twizzle)	(&)a4&a5&
Hop L	6
Ball dig R across L (with weight) Heel beat R	&a
Step L in place	7
Ball dig R in place (with weight) Heel beat R	&a
Ball dig L	8
Spring onto the balls of both feet with L foot in front of R	1
Toe clip R to L heel (using outside of R toe to outside of L heel)	&
Heel beat L	2
Step R	3
Shuffle L 3 times (6 beat Single twizzle)	(&)a4&a5&
Hop R	6
Ball dig L across R (with weight) Heel beat L	&a
Step R in place	7
Ball dig L in place (with weight) Heel beat L	&a
Ball dig R (with weight)	8

(vertical sidebar) **INTERMEDIATE**

Continued/

/continued

Variation –

Step L	1
Shuffle R twice (4 beat Single twizzle)	(&)a2&a
Hop L	3
Ball dig R across L (with weight) Heel beat R	&a
Step L in place	4
Ball dig R in place (with weight) Heel beat R	&a
Step L	5
Shuffle R twice (4 beat Single twizzle)	(&)a6&a
Hop L	7
Ball dig R across L (with weight) Heel beat R	&a
Step L in place	8
Ball dig R in place (with weight) Heel beat R	&a
Break – R	2 bars
Repeat all on opposite side	8 bars

INTERMEDIATE

77

Single twizzle, over & hop variation, clip toes & heels together & toe to heel clip

Step L	1
Shuffle R twice (4 beat Single twizzle)	(&)a2&a
Hop L	3
Ball dig R across L (with weight) Heel beat R	&a
Step L in place	4
Ball dig R in place (with weight) Heel beat R	&a
Heel dig L-R	5&
Clip toes together	a
Step L-R	6&
Clip heels together	&
Heel dig R	a
Heel dig L	7
Toe clip R to L heel	&
Step R behind L	a
Step L in place	8
Toe clip R to L heel	&
Heel beat L	a

INTERMEDIATE

Continued/

/continued

Step R	1
Shuffle L twice (4 beat Single twizzle)	(&)a2&a
Hop R	3
Ball dig L across R (with weight) Heel beat L	&a
Step R in place	4
Ball dig L in place (with weight) Heel beat L	&a
Heel dig R-L	5&
Clip toes together	a
Step R-L	6&
Clip heels together	&
Heel dig L	a
Heel dig R	7
Toe clip L to R heel	&
Step L behind R	a
Step R in place	8
Toe clip L to R heel	&
Heel beat R	a

INTERMEDIATE

continued/

TWIZZLES

/continued

Step L	1
Shuffle R twice (4 beat Single twizzle)	(&)a2&a
Hop L	3
Ball dig R across L (with weight) Heel beat R	&a
Step L in place	4
Ball dig R in place (with weight) Heel beat R	&a
Heel dig L-R	5&
Clip toes together	a
Step L-R	6&
Clip heels together	&
Heel dig R	a
Heel dig L	7
Toe clip R to L heel	&
Step R behind L	a
Step L in place	8
Toe clip R to L heel	&
Break – R commencing 'Heel beat L' instead of 'Step L' to continue break on the correct side	2 bars
Repeat all on opposite side	8 bars

I N T E R M E D I A T E (vertical sidebar)

80

Single twizzle, over & hop variation & stepping back

Step L	1
Shuffle R twice (4 beat Single twizzle)	(&)a2&a
Hop L	3
Ball dig R across L (with weight) Heel beat R	&a
Step L in place	4
Ball dig R in place (with weight) Heel beat R	&a
Step L	5
Shuffle R	&6
Hop L Heel beat L	&a
Step R behind L	7
Tap Step L	&8

Step R	1
Shuffle L twice (4 beat Single twizzle)	(&)a2&a
Hop R	3
Ball dig L across R (with weight) Heel beat L	&a
Step R in place	4
Ball dig L in place (with weight) Heel beat L	&a
Step R	5
Shuffle L	&6
Hop R Heel beat R	&a
Step L behind R	7
Tap Step R	&8

I N T E R M E D I A T E

Continued/

81

TWIZZLES

/continued

Step L	1
Shuffle R twice (4 beat Single twizzle)	(&)a2&a
Hop L	3
Ball dig R across L (with weight) Heel beat R	&a
Step L in place	4
Ball dig R in place (with weight) Heel beat R	&a
Step L	5
Shuffle R	&6
Hop L Heel beat L	&a
Step R behind L	7
Tap Step L	&8

Break – R commencing with 'Hop L' instead of
'Step L' to continue break on the correct side   2 bars

Repeat all on the opposite side   8 bars

Single twizzle, over & hop variation & stepping back (with variation)

Step L	1
Shuffle R twice (4 beat Single twizzle)	(&)a2&a
Hop L	3
Ball dig R across L (with weight) Heel beat R	&a
Step L in place	4
Ball dig R in place (with weight) Heel beat R	&a
Step L	5
Shuffle R	&6
Hop L Heel beat L	&a
Step R behind L	7
Tap Step L	&8
Step R	1
Shuffle L twice (4 beat Single twizzle)	(&)a2&a
Hop R	3
Ball dig L across R (with weight) Heel beat L	&a
Step R in place	4
Ball dig L in place (with weight) Heel beat L	&a
Step R	5
Shuffle L	&6
Hop R Heel beat R	&a
Step L behind R	7
Tap Step R	&8

INTERMEDIATE

Continued/

83

TWIZZLES

/continued

<u>Variation</u> –

Tap step L	&1
Shuffle R	&2
Hop L Heel beat L	&a
Step R behind L	3
Tap Step L	&4
Tap step R	&5
Shuffle L	&6
Hop R Heel beat R	&a
Step L behind R	7
Tap Step R	&8
Break – R	2 bars
Repeat all on opposite side	8 bars

I
N
T
E
R
M
E
D
I
A
T
E

Walking Monty (with variation)

Tap step L	&1
Shuffle R	&2
Ball dig R across (with weight) Heel beat R	&a
Step L in place	3
Tap step R by side of L	&4
Tap step L	&5
Ball dig R behind (with weight)	(&)a
Heel beat L	6
Shuffle R	&7
Ball dig R across (with weight) Heel beat R	&a
Step L in place	8
Tap step R	&1
Shuffle L	&2
Ball dig L across (with weight) Heel beat L	&a
Step R in place	3
Tap step L by side of R	&4
Tap step R	&5
Ball dig L behind (with weight)	(&)a
Heel beat R	6
Shuffle L	&7
Ball dig L across (with weight) Heel beat L	&a
Step R in place	8

I
N
T
E
R
M
E
D
I
A
T
E

Continued/

TWIZZLES

/continued

Variation –

Step L	1
Shuffle R twice (4 beat Single twizzle)	(&)a2&a
Ball dig R	3
Shuffle R twice (4 beat Single twizzle)	(&)a4&a
Step R	5
Shuffle L twice (4 beat Single twizzle)	(&)a6&a
Ball dig L	7
Shuffle L twice (4 beat Single twizzle)	(&)a8&a

Break – R   2 bars

Repeat all on opposite side   8 bars

<u>Toe to heel clips</u> (with variation)

Heel dig L	1
Toe clip R to L heel	&
Step R behind L	a
Step L in place	2
Toe clip R to L heel	&
Heel beat L	a
Heel dig R	3
Toe clip L to R heel	&
Step L behind R	a
Step R in place	4
Toe clip L to R heel	&
Heel beat R	a
Heel dig L	5
Toe clip R to L heel	&
Step R behind L	a
Step L in place	6
Toe clip R to L heel	&
Heel beat L	a
Shuffle R	7&
Heel beat L	a
Ball dig R in place	8

I N T E R M E D I A T E

Continued/

87

/continued

Heel dig R	1
Toe clip L to R heel	&
Step L behind R	a
Step R in place	2
Toe clip L to R heel	&
Heel beat R	a
Heel dig L	3
Toe clip R to L heel	&
Step R behind L	a
Step L in place	4
Toe clip R to L heel	&
Heel beat L	a
Heel dig R	5
Toe clip L to R heel	&
Step L behind R	a
Step R in place	6
Toe clip L to R heel	&
Heel beat R	a
Shuffle L	7&
Heel beat R	a
Ball dig L in place	8

INTERMEDIATE

continued/

/continued

<u>Variation</u> –

Heel dig L	1
Toe clip R to L heel	&
Step R behind L	a
Step L in place	2
Toe clip R to L heel	&
Heel beat L	a
Shuffle R	3&
Heel beat L	a
Ball dig R in place	4

Heel dig R	5
Toe clip L to R heel	&
Step L behind R	a
Step R in place	6
Toe clip L to R heel	&
Heel beat R	a
Shuffle L	7&
Heel beat R	a
Ball dig L in place	8

Break – R 2 bars

Repeat all on opposite side 8 bars

I
N
T
E
R
M
E
D
I
A
T
E

89

TOE TO
HEEL CLIPS

Stamp & toe to heel clip (with variation)

Step L		1
Straight tap R		2
Shuffle R	} Stamp R	&3
Ball dig R (with weight) Heel beat R		&a
Ball dig L		4

Heel dig L	5
Toe clip R to L heel	&
Step R behind L	a
Step L in place	6
Toe clip R to L heel	&
Heel beat L	a
Shuffle R	7&
Heel beat L	a
Ball dig R in place	8

Step R		1
Straight tap L		2
Shuffle L	} Stamp L	&3
Ball dig L (with weight) Heel beat L		&a
Ball dig R		4

Continued/

90

/continued

Heel dig R	5
Toe clip L to R heel	&
Step L behind R	a
Step R in place	6
Toe clip L to R heel	&
Heel beat R	a
Shuffle L	7&
Heel beat R	a
Ball dig L in place	8

Variation -

Heel dig L	1
Toe clip R to L heel	&
Step R behind L	a
Step L in place	2
Toe clip R to L heel	&
Heel beat L	a
Shuffle R	3&
Heel beat L	a
Ball dig R in place	4

INTERMEDIATE

continued/

TOE TO
HEEL CLIPS

/continued

Heel dig R	5
Toe clip L to R heel	&
Step L behind R	a
Step R in place	6
Toe clip L to R heel	&
Heel beat R	a
Shuffle L	7&
Heel beat R	a
Ball dig L in place	8

Break – R   2 bars

Repeat all on opposite side   8 bars

<u>Over & hop & toe to heel clip</u> (with variation)

Step L	1
Shuffle R Hop L	&a2
Ball dig R across L (with weight) Heel beat R	&a
Step L in place	3
Ball dig R in place (with weight) Heel beat R	&a
Ball dig L	4
Heel dig L	5
Toe clip R to L heel	&
Step R behind L	a
Step L in place	6
Toe clip R to L heel	&
Heel beat L	a
Shuffle R	7&
Heel beat L Ball dig R	a8
Step R	1
Shuffle L Hop R	&a2
Ball dig L across R (with weight) Heel beat L	&a
Step R in place	3
Ball dig L in place (with weight) Heel beat L	&a
Ball dig R	4
Heel dig R	5
Toe clip L to R heel	&
Step L behind R	a
Step R in place	6
Toe clip L to R heel	&
Heel beat R	a
Shuffle L	7&
Heel beat R Ball dig L	a8

Continued/

INTERMEDIATE

93

TOE TO
HEEL CLIPS

/continued

<u>Variation</u> –

Heel dig L	1
Toe clip R to L heel	&
Step R behind L	a
Step L in place	2
Toe clip R to L heel	&
Heel beat L	a
Shuffle R	3&
Heel beat L Ball dig R	a4
Heel dig R	5
Toe clip L to R heel	&
Step L behind R	a
Step R in place	6
Toe clip L to R heel	&
Heel beat R	a
Shuffle L	7&
Heel beat R Ball dig L	a8

Break – R   2 bars

Repeat all on opposite side   8 bars

94

Toe to heel clip & clip toes & heels together

(repeats 6 times on alternate sides)

Heel dig L	1
Toe clip R to L heel	&
Step R behind L	a
Step L in place	2
Toe clip R to L heel	&
Heel beat L	a
Heel dig R-L	3&
Clip toes together	a
Step R-L	4&
Clip heels together	a
Heel dig R	5
Toe clip L to R heel	&
Step L behind R	a
Step R in place	6
Toe clip L to R heel	&
Heel beat R	a
Heel dig L-R	7&
Clip toes together	a
Step L-R	8&
Clip heels together	a

I N T E R M E D I A T E

Continued/

95

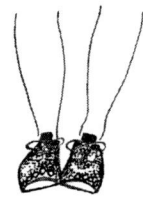

TOE TO
HEEL CLIPS

/continued

Heel dig L	1
Toe clip R to L heel	&
Step R behind L	a
Step L in place	2
Toe clip R to L heel	&
Heel beat L	a
Heel dig R-L	3&
Clip toes together	a
Step R-L	4&
Clip heels together	a
Heel dig R	5
Toe clip L to R heel	&
Step L behind R	a
Step R in place	6
Toe clip L to R heel	&
Heel beat R	a
Heel dig L-R	7&
Clip toes together	a
Step L-R	8&
Clip heels together	a

continued/

/continued

Heel dig L	1
Toe clip R to L heel	&
Step R behind L	a
Step L in place	2
Toe clip R to L heel	&
Heel beat L	a
Heel dig R-L	3&
Clip toes together	a
Step R-L	4&
Clip heels together	a
Heel dig R	5
Toe clip L to R heel	&
Step L behind R	a
Step R in place	6
Toe clip L to R heel	&
Heel beat R	a
Heel dig L-R	7&
Clip toes together	a
Step L-R	8&
Clip heels together	a
Break – R	2 bars

INTERMEDIATE

Repeat all on opposite side   8 bars

97

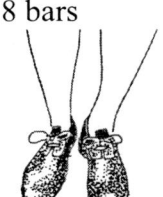

Double heel down & toe to heel clip

Step L	1
Heel dig R (no weight) Heel dig R (with weight)	&a
Step L	2
Shuffle R	&a
Step R	3
Heel dig L (no weight) Heel dig L (with weight)	&a
Step R	4
Shuffle L	&a
Heel dig L	5
Toe clip R to L heel	&
Step R behind L	a
Step L in place	6
Toe clip R to L heel	&
Heel beat L	a
Heel dig R	7
Toe clip L to R heel	&
Step L behind R	a
Step R in place	8
Toe clip L to R heel	&
Heel beat R	a

Continued/

/continued

Step L	1
Heel dig R (no weight) Heel dig R (with weight)	&a
Step L	2
Shuffle R	&a
Step R	3
Heel dig L (no weight) Heel dig L (with weight)	&a
Step R	4
Shuffle L	&a
Heel dig L	5
Toe clip R to L heel	&
Step R behind L	a
Step L in place	6
Toe clip R to L heel	&
Heel beat L	a
Heel dig R	7
Toe clip L to R heel	&
Step L behind R	a
Step R in place	8
Toe clip L to R heel	&
Heel beat R	a

INTERMEDIATE

continued/

99

TOE TO
HEEL CLIPS

/continued

Step L	1
Heel dig R (no weight) Heel dig R (with weight)	&a
Step L	2
Shuffle R	&a
Step R	3
Heel dig L (no weight) Heel dig L (with weight)	&a
Step R	4
Shuffle L	&a
Heel dig L	5
Toe clip R to L heel	&
Step R behind L	a
Step L in place	6
Toe clip R to L heel	&
Heel beat L	a
Heel dig R	7
Toe clip L to R heel	&
Step L behind R	a
Step R in place	8
Toe clip L to R heel	&
Heel beat R	a
Break – R	2 bars
Repeat all on opposite side	8 bars

INTERMEDIATE

Stepping over & toe to heel clips stepping onto ball of foot
(with variation)

Step L	1
Shuffle R	&2
Ball dig R across L (with weight) Heel beat R	&a
Step L in place	3
Tap step R by side of L	&4
Tap step L	&5
Toe clip R to L heel (using inner side of both feet)	&
Step R behind L	a
Step L in place	6
Toe clip R to L heel (using outer side of both feet)	&
Step R in place	a
Step L in place	7
Toe clip R to L heel (using inner side of both feet)	&
Step R behind L	a
Step L in place	8
Toe clip R to L heel (using outer side of both feet)	&
Heel beat L	a

I
N
T
E
R
M
E
D
I
A
T
E

Continued/

TOE TO
HEEL CLIPS

/continued

Step R	1
Shuffle L	&2
Ball dig L across R (with weight) Heel beat L	&a
Step R in place	3
Tap step L by side of R	&4
Tap step R	&5
Toe clip L to R heel (using inner side of both feet)	&
Step L behind R	a
Step R in place	6
Toe clip L to R heel (using outer side of both feet)	&
Step L in place	a
Step R in place	7
Toe clip L to R heel (using inner side of both feet)	&
Step L behind R	a
Step R in place	8
Toe clip L to R heel (using outer side of both feet)	&
Heel beat R	a

continued/

I
N
T
E
R
M
E
D
I
A
T
E

Variation –

Step L	1
Toe clip R to L heel (using inner side of both feet)	&
Step R behind L	a
Step L in place	2
Toe clip R to L heel (using outer side of both feet)	&
Step R in place	a
Step L in place	3
Toe clip R to L heel (using inner side of both feet)	&
Step R behind L	a
Step L in place	4
Toe clip R to L heel (using outer side of both feet)	&
Heel beat L	a
Step R	5
Toe clip L to R heel (using inner side of both feet)	&
Step L behind R	a
Step R in place	6
Toe clip L to R heel (using outer side of both feet)	&
Step L in place	a
Step R in place	7
Toe clip L to R heel (using inner side of both feet)	&
Step L behind R	a
Step R in place	8
Toe clip L to R heel (using outer side of both feet)	&
Heel beat R	a
Break – R	2 bars
Repeat all on opposite side	8 bars

I
N
T
E
R
M
E
D
I
A
T
E

103

TOE TO
HEEL CLIPS

Toe to heel clips stepping onto ball of foot & **over & hop**

Tap step L	&1
Toe clip R to L heel (using inner side of both feet)	&
Step R behind L	a
Step L in place	2
Toe clip R to L heel (using outer side of both feet)	&
Step R in place	a
Step L in place	3
Toe clip R to L heel (using inner side of both feet)	&
Step R behind L	a
Step L in place	4
Toe clip R to L heel (using outer side of both feet)	&
Heel beat L	5
Shuffle R Hop L	&a6
Ball dig R across L (with weight) Heel beat R	&a
Step L in place	7
Ball dig R in place (with weight) Heel beat R	&a
Ball dig L (with weight)	8

Continued/

/continued

Tap step R	&1
Toe clip L to R heel (using inner side of both feet)	&
Step L behind R	a
Step R in place	2
Toe clip L to R heel (using outer side of both feet)	&
Step L in place	a
Step R in place	3
Toe clip L to R heel (using inner side of both feet)	&
Step L behind R	a
Step R in place	4
Toe clip L to R heel (using outer side of both feet)	&
Heel beat R	5
Shuffle L Hop R	&a6
Ball dig L across R (with weight) Heel beat L	&a
Step R in place	7
Ball dig L in place (with weight) Heel beat L	&a
Ball dig R (with weight)	8

INTERMEDIATE

continued/

/continued

Tap step L	&1
Toe clip R to L heel (using inner side of both feet)	&
Step R behind L	a
Step L in place	2
Toe clip R to L heel (using outer side of both feet)	&
Step R in place	a
Step L in place	3
Toe clip R to L heel (using inner side of both feet)	&
Step R behind L	a
Step L in place	4
Toe clip R to L heel (using outer side of both feet)	&
Heel beat L	5
Shuffle R Hop L	&a6
Ball dig R across L (with weight) Heel beat R	&a
Step L in place	7
Ball dig R in place (with weight) Heel beat R	&a
Ball dig L	8
Break – R	2 bars
Repeat all on opposite side	8 bars

I
N
T
E
R
M
E
D
I
A
T
E

106

<u>Double shuffle, clip toes & heels together & toe</u>
<u>to heel clip</u>
(with variation)

Step L	1
Shuffle R Hop L Shuffle R	&a2&a
Step R	3
Shuffle L Hop R Shuffle L	&a4&a
Heel dig L-R	5&
Clip toes together	a
Step L-R	6&
Clip heels together	a
Heel dig L	7
Toe clip R to L heel	&
Step R behind L	a
Step L in place	8
Toe clip R to L heel	&
Heel beat L	a

I
N
T
E
R
M
E
D
I
A
T
E

Continued/

TOE TO
HEEL CLIPS

/continued

Step R	1
Shuffle L Hop R Shuffle L	&a2&a
Step L	3
Shuffle R Hop L Shuffle R	&a4&a
Heel dig R-L	5&
Clip toes together	a
Step R-L	6&
Clip heels together	a
Heel dig R	7
Toe clip L to R heel	&
Step L behind R	a
Step R in place	8
Toe clip L to R heel	&
Heel beat R	a

continued/

/continued

Variation -

Heel dig L-R	1&
Clip toes together	a
Step L-R	2&
Clip heels together	a
Heel dig L	3
Toe clip R to L heel	&
Step R behind L	a
Step L in place	4
Toe clip R to L heel	&
Heel beat L	a
Heel dig R-L	5&
Clip toes together	a
Step R-L	6&
Clip heels together	a
Heel dig R	7
Toe clip L to R heel	&
Step L behind R	a
Step R in place	8
Toe clip L to R heel	&
Heel beat R	a
Break – R	2 bars
Repeat all on opposite side	8 bars

INTERMEDIATE

109

TOE TO
HEEL CLIPS

<u>Double shuffle, over & hop variation & toe to heel clip</u>
(with variation)

INTERMEDIATE

Step L	1
Shuffle R Hop L Shuffle R	&a2&a
Hop L	3
Ball dig R across (with weight) Heel beat R	&a
Step L	4
Ball dig R in place (with weight) Heel beat R	&a
Heel dig L	5
Toe clip R to L heel	&
Step R behind L	a
Step L in place	6
Toe clip R to L heel	&
Heel beat L	a
Shuffle R	7&
Heel beat L	a
Ball dig R in place	8

Continued/

/continued

Step R	1
Shuffle L Hop R Shuffle L	&a2&a
Hop R	3
Ball dig L across (with weight) Heel beat L	&a
Step R	4
Ball dig L in place (with weight) Heel beat L	&a
Heel dig R	5
Toe clip L to R heel	&
Step L behind R	a
Step R in place	6
Toe clip L to R heel	&
Heel beat R	a
Shuffle L	7&
Heel beat R	a
Ball dig L in place	8

I
N
T
E
R
M
E
D
I
A
T
E

continued/

111

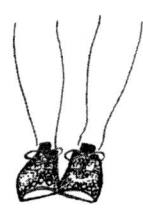

TOE TO
HEEL CLIPS

/continued

<u>Variation</u> –

Spring L Shuffle R		1&&
Step R-L		a2
Shuffle R	Double treble R	&a
Hop L Shuffle R		3&&
Step R-L		a4
Shuffle R		&a
Spring R Shuffle L		5&&
Step L-R		a6
Shuffle L	Double treble L	&a
Hop R Shuffle L		7&&
Step L-R		a8
Shuffle L		&a
Break – R		2 bars
Repeat all on opposite side		8 bars

Clip toes & heels together, toe to heel clip & over & hop

Heel dig L-R	&1
Clip toes together	&
Step L-R	a2
Clip heels together	&
Heel dig L	3
Toe clip R to L heel	&
Step R behind L	a
Step L in place	4
Toe clip R to L heel	&
Heel beat L	5
Shuffle R Hop L	&a6
Ball dig R across L (with weight) Heel beat R	&a
Step L in place	7
Ball dig R in place (with weight) Heel beat R	&a
Ball dig L (with weight)	8

I
N
T
E
R
M
E
D
I
A
T
E

Continued/

113

TOE TO
HEEL CLIPS

/continued

Heel dig R-L	&1
Clip toes together	&
Step R-L	a2
Clip heels together	&
Heel dig R	3
Toe clip L to R heel	&
Step L behind R	a
Step R in place	4
Toe clip L to R heel	&
Heel beat R	5
Shuffle L Hop R	&a6
Ball dig L across R (with weight) Heel beat L	&a
Step R in place	7
Ball dig L in place (with weight) Heel beat L	&a
Ball dig R (with weight)	8

continued/

/continued

Heel dig L-R	&1
Clip toes together	&
Step L-R	a2
Clip heels together	&
Heel dig L	3
Toe clip R to L heel	&
Step R behind L	a
Step L in place	4
Toe clip R to L heel	&
Heel beat L	5
Shuffle R Hop L	&a6
Ball dig R across L (with weight) Heel beat R	&a
Step L in place	7
Ball dig R in place (with weight) Heel beat R	&a
Ball dig L	8
Break – R	2 bars
Repeat all on opposite side	8 bars

I
N
T
E
R
M
E
D
I
A
T
E

115

Shuffle across, toe to heel clip & clip toes & heels together

I
N
T
E
R
M
E
D
I
A
T
E

Tap step L	&1
Shuffle R Heel beat L (turning R knee out bring R heel across L)	&a2
Tap step R	&3
Shuffle L Heel beat R (turning L knee out bring L heel across R)	&a4
Heel dig L	5
Toe clip R to L heel	&
Step R behind L	a
Step L in place	6
Toe clip R to L heel	&
Heel beat L	a
Heel dig R-L	7&
Clip toes together	a
Step R-L	8&
Clip heels together	&

Continued/

/continued

Tap step R	a1
Shuffle L Heel beat R (turning L knee out bring L heel across R)	&a2
Tap step L	&3
Shuffle R Heel beat L (turning R knee out bring R heel across L)	&a4
Heel dig R	5
Toe clip L to R heel	&
Step L behind R	a
Step R in place	6
Toe clip L to R heel	&
Heel beat R	a
Heel dig L-R	7&
Clip toes together	a
Step L-R	8&
Clip heels together	&

I N T E R M E D I A T E

/continued

117

TOE TO
HEEL CLIPS

/continued

Tap step L	a1
Shuffle R Heel beat L (turning R knee out bring R heel across L)	&a2
Tap step R	&3
Shuffle L Heel beat R (turning L knee out bring L heel across R)	&a4
Heel dig L	5
Toe clip R to L heel	&
Step R behind L	a
Step L in place	6
Toe clip R to L heel	&
Heel beat L	a
Heel dig R-L	7&
Clip toes together	a
Step R-L	8&
Clip heels together	a
Break – R	2 bars
Repeat all on opposite side	8 bars

Toe to heel clips & over & hop
(with variation)

Heel dig L	1
Toe clip R to L heel	&
Step R behind L	a
Step L in place	2
Toe clip R to L heel	&
Heel beat L	a
Heel dig R	3
Toe clip L to R heel	&
Step L behind R	a
Step R in place	4
Toe clip L to R heel	&
Heel beat R	a
Step L	5
Shuffle R Hop L	&a6
Ball dig R across L (with weight) Heel beat R	&a
Step L in place	7
Ball dig R in place (with weight) Heel beat R	&a
Ball dig L (with weight)	8

INTERMEDIATE

Continued/

119

TOE TO
HEEL CLIPS

/continued

Heel dig R	1
Toe clip L to R heel	&
Step L behind R	a
Step R in place	2
Toe clip L to R heel	&
Heel beat R	a
Heel dig L	3
Toe clip R to L heel	&
Step R behind L	a
Step L in place	4
Toe clip R to L heel	&
Heel beat L	a
Step R	5
Shuffle L Hop R	&a6
Ball dig L across R (with weight) Heel beat L	&a
Step R in place	7
Ball dig L in place (with weight) Heel beat L	&a
Ball dig R (with weight)	8

INTERMEDIATE

/continued

/continued

Variation -

Step L	1
Shuffle R Hop L	&a2
Ball dig R across L (with weight) Heel beat R	&a
Step L in place	3
Ball dig R in place (with weight) Heel beat R	&a
Heel dig L-R Clip toes together	4&a
Heel dig L	5
Toe clip R to L heel	&
Step R behind L	a
Step L in place	6
Toe clip R to L heel	&
Heel beat L	a
Heel dig R-L	7&
Clip toes together	a
Step R-L	8&
Clip heels together	a
Break – R	2 bars
Repeat all on opposite side	8 bars

I
N
T
E
R
M
E
D
I
A
T
E

121

Toe to heel clips & over & hop
(with alternative variation)

Heel dig L	1
Toe clip R to L heel	&
Step R behind L	a
Step L in place	2
Toe clip R to L heel	&
Heel beat L	a
Heel dig R	3
Toe clip L to R heel	&
Step L behind R	a
Step R in place	4
Toe clip L to R heel	&
Heel beat R	a
Step L	5
Shuffle R Hop L	&a6
Ball dig R across L (with weight) Heel beat R	&a
Step L in place	7
Ball dig R in place (with weight) Heel beat R	&a
Ball dig L (with weight)	8

Continued/

I
N
T
E
R
M
E
D
I
A
T
E

/continued

Heel dig R	1
Toe clip L to R heel	&
Step L behind R	a
Step R in place	2
Toe clip L to R heel	&
Heel beat R	a
Heel dig L	3
Toe clip R to L heel	&
Step R behind L	a
Step L in place	4
Toe clip R to L heel	&
Heel beat L	a
Step R	5
Shuffle L Hop R	&a6
Ball dig L across R (with weight) Heel beat L	&a
Step R in place	7
Ball dig L in place (with weight) Heel beat L	&a
Ball dig R (with weight)	8

INTERMEDIATE

continued/

TOE TO
HEEL CLIPS

/continued

<u>Variation</u> -

Heel dig L-R	&1
Clip toes together	&
Step L-R	a2
Clip heels together	&
Heel dig L	3
Toe clip R to L heel	&
Step R behind L	a
Step L in place	4
Toe clip R to L heel	&
Heel beat L	&
Heel dig R-L	a5
Clip toes together	&
Step R-L	a6
Clip heels together	&
Heel dig R	7
Toe clip L to R heel	&
Step L behind R	a
Step R in place	8
Toe clip L to R heel	&
Heel beat R	a
Break – R	2 bars
Repeat all on opposite side	8 bars

Toe to heel clips & double treble

Heel dig L	1
Toe clip R to L heel	&
Step R behind L	a
Step L in place	2
Toe clip R to L heel	&
Heel beat L	a
Heel dig R	3
Toe clip L to R heel	&
Step L behind R	a
Step R in place	4
Toe clip L to R heel	&
Heel beat R	a

Spring L Shuffle R ⎫   5&&
Step R-L   a6
Shuffle R   ⎬ Double treble R   &a
Hop L Shuffle R   7&&
Step R-L   a8
Shuffle R ⎭   &a

I N T E R M E D I A T E

Continued/

125

/continued

Heel dig R	1
Toe clip L to R heel	&
Step L behind R	a
Step R in place	2
Toe clip L to R heel	&
Heel beat R	a
Heel dig L	3
Toe clip R to L heel	&
Step R behind L	a
Step L in place	4
Toe clip R to L heel	&
Heel beat L	a

Spring R Shuffle L		5&&
Step L-R		a6
Shuffle L	Double treble L	&a
Hop R Shuffle L		7&&
Step L-R		a8
Shuffle L		&a

**I
N
T
E
R
M
E
D
I
A
T
E**

continued/

/continued

Heel dig L	1
Toe clip R to L heel	&
Step R behind L	a
Step L in place	2
Toe clip R to L heel	&
Heel beat L	a
Heel dig R	3
Toe clip L to R heel	&
Step L behind R	a
Step R in place	4
Toe clip L to R heel	&
Heel beat R	a

Spring L Shuffle R	⎫	5&&
Step R-L	⎪	a6
Shuffle R	⎬ Double treble R	&a
Hop L Shuffle R	⎪	7&&
Step R-L	⎪	a8
Shuffle R	⎭	&a

Break – R commencing with 'Hop L' instead of
'Step L' to continue break on the correct side   2 bars

Repeat all on opposite side   8 bars

I
N
T
E
R
M
E
D
I
A
T
E

127

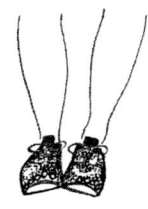

<u>Toe to heel clips & double treble</u>
(with variation)

Heel dig L	1
Toe clip R to L heel	&
Step R behind L	a
Step L in place	2
Toe clip R to L heel	&
Heel beat L	a
Heel dig R	3
Toe clip L to R heel	&
Step L behind R	a
Step R in place	4
Toe clip L to R heel	&
Heel beat R	a

Spring L Shuffle R		5&&
Step R-L		a6
Shuffle R	Double treble R	&a
Hop L Shuffle R		7&&
Step R-L		a8
Shuffle R		&a

Continued/

128

/continued

Heel dig R	1
Toe clip L to R heel	&
Step L behind R	a
Step R in place	2
Toe clip L to R heel	&
Heel beat R	a
Heel dig L	3
Toe clip R to L heel	&
Step R behind L	a
Step L in place	4
Toe clip R to L heel	&
Heel beat L	a

Spring R Shuffle L   ⎫   5&&
Step L-R   ⎪   a6
Shuffle L   ⎬ Double treble L &a
Hop R Shuffle L   ⎪   7&&
Step L-R   ⎪   a8
Shuffle L   ⎭   &a

INTERMEDIATE

continued/

129

TOE TO
HEEL CLIPS

/continued

<u>Variation</u> –

Spring L Shuffle R		1&&
Step R-L		a2
Shuffle R	Double treble R	&a
Hop L Shuffle R		3&&
Step R-L		a4
Shuffle R		&a
Spring R Shuffle L		5&&
Step L-R		a6
Shuffle L	Double treble L	&a
Hop R Shuffle L		7&&
Step L-R		a8
Shuffle L		&a

Break – R   2 bars

Repeat all on opposite side   8 bars

Stamp & heel to toe clip
(with variation)

Step L	1
Straight tap R	2
Shuffle R	&3
Ball dig R (with weight) Heel beat R	&a
Ball dig L	4
Heel dig L	5
Heel clip R to L toe (using inner side of heel)	&
Ball beat L	a
Step R across L	6
Toe clip L to R heel (using outer side of both feet)	&
Heel beat R	a
Shuffle L	7&
Heel beat R	a
Ball dig L in place (with weight)	8

I
N
T
E
R
M
E
D
I
A
T
E

Continued/

131

HEEL TO
TOE CLIPS

/continued

Step R	1
Straight tap L	2
Shuffle L	&3
Ball dig L (with weight) Heel beat L	&a
Ball dig R	4
Heel dig R	5
Heel clip L to R toe (using inner side of heel)	&
Ball beat R	a
Step L across R	6
Toe clip R to L heel (using outer side of both feet)	&
Heel beat L	a
Shuffle R	7&
Heel beat L	a
Ball dig R in place (with weight)	8

INTERMEDIATE

continued/

/continued

Variation –

Heel dig L	1
Heel clip R to L toe (using inner side of heel)	&
Ball beat L	a
Step R across L	2
Toe clip L to R heel (using outer side of both feet)	&
Heel beat R	a
Shuffle L	3&
Heel beat R	a
Ball dig L in place (with weight)	4
Heel dig R	5
Heel clip L to R toe (using inner side of heel)	&
Ball beat R	a
Step L across R	6
Toe clip R to L heel (using outer side of both feet)	&
Heel beat L	a
Shuffle R	7&
Heel beat L	a
Ball dig R in place (with weight)	8
Break – R	2 bars
Repeat all on opposite side	8 bars

I
N
T
E
R
M
E
D
I
A
T
E

133

Toe to heel clips & heel to toe clip
(with variation)

Heel dig L	1
Toe clip R to L heel	&
Step R behind L	a
Step L in place	2
Toe clip R to L heel (using outer side of both feet)	&
Heel beat L	a
Heel dig R	3
Toe clip L to R heel	&
Step L behind R	a
Step R in place	4
Toe clip L to R heel (using outer side of both feet)	&
Heel beat R	a
Heel dig L	5
Heel clip R to L toe (using inner side of heel)	&
Ball beat L	a
Step R across L	6
Toe clip L to R heel (using outer side of both feet)	&
Heel beat R	a
Shuffle L	7&
Heel beat R	a
Ball dig L in place (with weight)	8

I N T E R M E D I A T E

Continued/

134

/continued

Heel dig R	1
Toe clip L to R heel	&
Step L behind R	a
Step R in place	2
Toe clip L to R heel (using outer side of both feet)	&
Heel beat R	a
Heel dig L	3
Toe clip R to L heel (using inner side of heel)	&
Step R behind L	a
Step L in place	4
Toe clip R to L heel (using outer side of both feet)	&
Heel beat L	a
Heel dig R	5
Heel clip L to R toe (using inner side of heel)	&
Ball beat R	a
Step L across R	6
Toe clip R to L heel (using outer side of both feet)	&
Heel beat L	a
Shuffle R	7&
Heel beat L	a
Ball dig R in place (with weight)	8

I
N
T
E
R
M
E
D
I
A
T
E

/continued

135

HEEL TO
TOE CLIPS

/continued

<u>Variation</u> –

Heel dig L	1
Heel clip R to L toe (using inner side of heel)	&
Ball beat L	a
Step R across L	2
Toe clip L to R heel (using outer side of both feet)	&
Heel beat R	a
Shuffle L	3&
Heel beat R	a
Ball dig L in place (with weight)	4
Heel dig R	5
Heel clip L to R toe (using inner side of heel)	&
Ball beat R	a
Step L across R	6
Toe clip R to L heel (using outer side of both feet)	&
Heel beat L	a
Shuffle R	7&
Heel beat L	a
Ball dig R in place (with weight)	8
Break – R	2 bars
Repeat all on opposite side	8 bars

I
N
T
E
R
M
E
D
I
A
T
E

Double heel down, clip toes & heels together & heel to toe clip

Step L	1
Heel dig R (no weight) Heel dig R (with weight)	&a
Step L	2
Shuffle R	&a
Step R	3
Heel dig L (no weight) Heel dig L (with weight)	&a
Step R	4
Shuffle L	&a
Heel dig L-R	5&
Clip toes together	a
Step L-R	6&
Clip heels together	a
Heel dig L	7
Heel clip R to L toe (using inner side of heel)	&
Ball beat L	a
Step R across L	8
Toe clip L to R heel (using outer side of both feet)	&

INTERMEDIATE

Continued/

137

/continued

Heel beat R	1
Heel dig L (no weight) Heel dig L (with weight)	&a
Step R	2
Shuffle L	&a
Step L	3
Heel dig R (no weight) Heel dig R (with weight)	&a
Step L	4
Shuffle R	&a
Heel dig R-L	5&
Clip toes together	a
Step R-L	6&
Clip heels together	a
Heel dig R	7
Heel clip L to R toe (using inner side of heel)	&
Ball beat R	a
Step L across R	8
Toe clip R to L heel (using outer side of both feet)	&

continued/

INTERMEDIATE

/continued

Heel beat L	1
Heel dig R (no weight) Heel dig R (with weight)	&a
Step L	2
Shuffle R	&a
Step R	3
Heel dig L (no weight) Heel dig L (with weight)	&a
Step R	4
Shuffle L	&a
Heel dig L-R	5&
Clip toes together	a
Step L-R	6&
Clip heels together	a
Heel dig L	7
Heel clip R to L toe (using inner side of heel)	&
Ball beat L	a
Step R across L	8
Toe clip L to R heel (using outer side of both feet)	&
Heel beat R	a
Break – R	2 bars
Repeat all on opposite side	8 bars

INTERMEDIATE

139

Toe to heel clip, heel to toe clip & over & hop

Heel dig L	1
Toe clip R to L heel	&
Step R behind L	a
Step L in place	2
Toe clip R to L heel (using outer side of both feet)	&
Heel beat L	a
Forward tap R	3
Heel clip R to L toe (using inner side of heel)	&
Ball beat L	a
Step R across L	4
Toe clip L to R heel (using outer side of both feet)	&
Heel beat R	a
Step L	5
Shuffle R Hop L	&a6
Ball dig R across L (with weight) Heel beat R	&a
Step L in place	7
Ball dig R in place (with weight) Heel beat R	&a
Ball dig L (with weight)	8

Continued/

/continued

Heel dig R	1
Toe clip L to R heel	&
Step L behind R	a
Step R in place	2
Toe clip L to R heel (using outer side of both feet)	&
Heel beat R	a
Forward tap L	3
Heel clip L to R toe (using inner side of heel)	&
Ball beat R	a
Step L across R	4
Toe clip R to L heel (using outer side of both feet)	&
Heel beat L	a
Step R	5
Shuffle L Hop R	&a6
Ball dig L across R (with weight) Heel beat L	&a
Step R in place	7
Ball dig L in place (with weight) Heel beat L	&a
Ball dig R (with weight)	8

I N T E R M E D I A T E

continued/

141

HEEL TO
TOE CLIPS

/continued

Heel dig L	1
Toe clip R to L heel	&
Step R behind L	a
Step L in place	2
Toe clip R to L heel (using outer side of both feet)	&
Heel beat L	a
Forward tap R	3
Heel clip R to L toe (using inner side of heel)	&
Ball beat L	a
Step R across L	4
Toe clip L to R heel (using outer side of both feet)	&
Heel beat R	a
Step L	5
Shuffle R Hop L	&a6
Ball dig R across L (with weight) Heel beat R	&a
Step L in place	7
Ball dig R in place (with weight) Heel beat R	&a
Ball dig L	8
Break – R	2 bars
Repeat all on opposite side	8 bars

Toe to heel clip, heel to toe clip & stepping back

Heel dig L	1
Toe clip R to L heel	&
Step R behind L	a
Step L in place	2
Toe clip R to L heel (using outer side of both feet)	&
Heel beat L	a
Forward tap R	3
Heel clip R to L toe (using inner side of heel)	&
Ball beat L	a
Step R across L	4
Toe clip L to R heel (using outer side of both feet)	&
Heel beat R	a
Step L	5
Shuffle R	&6
Hop L Heel beat L Step R behind L	&a7
Tap Step L	&8

INTERMEDIATE

Continued/

143

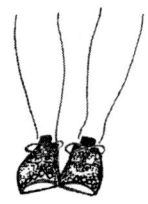

/continued

Heel dig R	1
Toe clip L to R heel	&
Step L behind R	a
Step R in place	2
Toe clip L to R heel (using outer side of both feet)	&
Heel beat R	a
Forward tap L	3
Heel clip L to R toe (using inner side of heel)	&
Ball beat R	a
Step L across R	4
Toe clip R to L heel (using outer side of both feet)	&
Heel beat L	a
Step R	5
Shuffle L	&6
Hop R Heel beat R Step L behind R	&a7
Tap Step R	&8

I N T E R M E D I A T E

continued/

/continued

Heel dig L	1
Toe clip R to L heel	&
Step R behind L	a
Step L in place	2
Toe clip R to L heel (using outer side of both feet)	&
Heel beat L	a
Forward tap R	3
Heel clip R to L toe (using inner side of heel)	&
Ball beat L	a
Step R across L	4
Toe clip L to R heel (using outer side of both feet)	&
Heel beat R	a
Step L	5
Shuffle R	&6
Hop L Heel beat L Step R behind L	&a7
Tap Step L	&8
Break – R commencing with 'Hop L' instead of 'Step L' to continue break on the correct side	2 bars
Repeat all on opposite side	8 bars

INTERMEDIATE

145

SINGLE &
DOUBLE
JUMPS

Single jump & stepping back (with variation)

Spring onto the balls of both feet with R foot in front of L	1
Tap step R	&2
Tap step L	&3
Tap step R	&4

Tap step L		&5
Shuffle R		&6
Hop L Heel beat L	Stepping back R	&a
Step R behind L		7
Tap step L		&8

Spring onto the balls of both feet with L foot in front of R	1
Tap step L	&2
Tap step R	&3
Tap step L	&4

Tap step R		&5
Shuffle L		&6
Hop R Heel beat R	Stepping back L	&a
Step L behind R		7
Tap step R		&8

Continued/

INTERMEDIATE

/continued

Variation -

Tap step L	⎫	&1
Shuffle R	⎪	&2
Hop L Heel beat L	⎬ Stepping back R	&a
Step R behind L	⎪	3
Tap step L	⎭	&4

Tap step R	⎫	&5
Shuffle L	⎪	&6
Hop R Heel beat R	⎬ Stepping back L	&a
Step L behind R	⎪	7
Tap step R	⎭	&8

Break – R   2 bars

Repeat all on opposite side   8 bars

INTERMEDIATE

147

Single jump, shuffle, clip toes together & first military

Spring onto the balls of both feet with R foot in front of L	1
Toe clip L to R heel (using outside of L toe to outside of R heel)	&
Heel beat R	2
Shuffle L	&3
Heel dig L-R	&a
Clip toes together	4
Tap step L	&5
Shuffle R	&6
Ball dig R (with weight) Heel beat R	&7
Shuffle L	&&
Ball dig L (with weight) Heel beat L	a8

Continued/

148

/continued

Spring onto the balls of both feet with L foot in front of R	1
Toe clip R to L heel (using outside of R toe to outside of L heel)	&
Heel beat L	2
Shuffle R	&3
Heel dig R-L	&a
Clip toes together	4
Tap step R	&5
Shuffle L	&6
Ball dig L (with weight) Heel beat L	&7
Shuffle R	&&
Ball dig R (with weight) Heel beat R	a8

INTERMEDIATE

continued/

149

SINGLE &
DOUBLE
 JUMPS

/continued

Spring onto the balls of both feet with R foot in front of L	1
Toe clip L to R heel (using outside of L toe to outside of R heel)	&
Heel beat R	2
Shuffle L	&3
Heel dig L-R	&a
Clip toes together	4
Tap step L	&5
Shuffle R	&6
Ball dig R (with weight) Heel beat R	&7
Shuffle L	&&
Ball dig L (with weight) Heel beat L	a8
Break R commencing with 'Hop L' instead of 'Step L' to continue break on the correct side	2 bars
Repeat all on opposite side	8 bars

Single jump, shuffle, clip toes together & toe to heel clip

Spring onto the balls of both feet with R foot in front of L	1
Toe clip L to R heel (using outside of L toe to outside of R heel)	&
Heel beat R	2
Shuffle L	&3
Heel dig L-R	&4
Clip toes together	&
Heel dig L	5
Toe clip R to L heel	&
Step R behind L	a
Step L in place	6
Toe clip R to L heel	&
Heel beat L	a
Shuffle R	7&
Heel beat L	a
Ball dig R in place	8

I N T E R M E D I A T E

Continued/

151

SINGLE &
DOUBLE
JUMPS

/continued

Spring onto the balls of both feet with L foot in front of R	1
Toe clip R to L heel (using outside of R toe to outside of L heel)	&
Heel beat L	2
Shuffle R	&3
Heel dig R-L	&4
Clip toes together	&
Heel dig R	5
Toe clip L to R heel	&
Step L behind R	a
Step R in place	6
Toe clip L to R heel	&
Heel beat R	a
Shuffle L	7&
Heel beat R	a
Ball dig L in place	8

continued/

Left margin vertical text: INTERMEDIATE

/continued

Spring onto the balls of both feet with **R** foot in front of L	1
Toe clip L to R heel (using outside of L toe to outside of R heel)	&
Heel beat R	2
Shuffle L	&3
Heel dig L-R	&4
Clip toes together	&
Heel dig L	5
Toe clip R to L heel	&
Step R behind L	a
Step L in place	6
Toe clip R to L heel	&
Heel beat L	a
Shuffle R	7&
Heel beat L	a
Ball dig R in place (with weight)	8
Break – R	2 bars
Repeat all on opposite side	8 bars

INTERMEDIATE

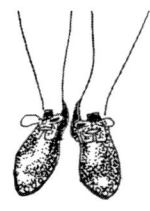

153

Single shuffles, single jump & clip toes & heels together

Step L	1
Shuffle R Step R	&a2
Shuffle L Step L	&a3
Spring onto both feet with R foot in front of L	4
Tap step R	&5
Tap step L	&6
Heel dig R Heel dig L	&7
Clip toes together	&
Step onto the balls of the feet R-L	a8
Clip heels together	&
Step R	1
Shuffle L Step L	&a2
Shuffle R Step R	&a3
Spring onto both feet with L foot in front of R	4
Tap step L	&5
Tap step R	&6
Heel dig L Heel dig R	&7
Clip toes together	&
Step onto the balls of the feet L-R	a8
Clip heels together	&

Continued/

I N T E R M E D I A T E

continued/

Step L	1
Shuffle R Step R	&a2
Shuffle L Step L	&a3
Spring onto both feet with R foot in front of L	4
Tap step R	&5
Tap step L	&6
Heel dig R Heel dig L	&7
Clip toes together	&
Step onto the balls of the feet R-L	a8
Clip heels together	&

Break – R   2 bars

Repeat all on opposite side   8 bars

I
N
T
E
R
M
E
D
I
A
T
E

Double jump & clip toes & heels together

INTERMEDIATE

Spring onto the balls of both feet with R foot in front of L	1
Spring onto the balls of both feet with L foot in front of R	2
Tap step L	&3
Tap step R	&4
Heel dig L Heel dig R	&a
Clip toes together	5
Step L-R	&a
Clip heels together	6
Heel dig L Heel dig R	&a
Clip toes together	7
Step L-R	&a
Clip heels together	8

Continued/

/continued

Spring onto the balls of both feet with L foot in front of R	1
Spring onto the balls of both feet with R foot in front of L	2
Tap step R	&3
Tap step L	&4
Heel dig R Heel dig L	&a
Clip toes together	5
Step R-L	&a
Clip heels together	6
Heel dig R Heel dig L	&a
Clip toes together	7
Step R-L	&a
Clip heels together	8

INTERMEDIATE

continued/

157

SINGLE &
DOUBLE
JUMPS

/continued

Spring onto the balls of both feet with R foot in front of L	1
Spring onto the balls of both feet with L foot in front of R	2
Tap step L	&3
Tap step R	&4
Heel dig L Heel dig R	&a
Clip toes together	5
Step L-R	&a
Clip heels together	6
Heel dig L Heel dig R	&a
Clip toes together	7
Step L-R	&a
Clip heels together	8
Break – R	2 bars
	8 bars
Repeat all on opposite side	

INTERMEDIATE

Double jump & toe to heel clip

Spring onto the balls of both feet with R foot in front of L	1
Spring onto the balls of both feet with L foot in front of R	2
Tap step L	&3
Tap step R	&4
Heel dig L	5
Toe clip R to L heel	&
Step R behind L	a
Step L in place	6
Toe clip R to L heel	&
Heel beat L	a
Shuffle R	7&
Heel beat L	a
Ball dig R in place	8

INTERMEDIATE

Continued/

159

/continued

Spring onto the balls of both feet with L foot in front of R	1
Spring onto the balls of both feet with R foot in front of L	2
Tap step R	&3
Tap step L	&4
Heel dig R	5
Toe clip L to R heel	&
Step L behind R	a
Step R in place	6
Toe clip L to R heel	&
Heel beat R	a
Shuffle L	7&
Heel beat R	a
Ball dig L in place	8

I N T E R M E D I A T E

continued/

/continued

Spring onto the balls of both feet with R foot in front of L	1
Spring onto the balls of both feet with L foot in front of R	2
Tap step L	&3
Tap step R	&4
Heel dig L	5
Toe clip R to L heel	&
Step R behind L	a
Step L in place	6
Toe clip R to L heel	&
Heel beat L	a
Shuffle R	7&
Heel beat L	a
Ball dig R in place (with weight)	8
Break R	2 bars
Repeat all on opposite side	8 bars

INTERMEDIATE

161

<u>Double jump & first military</u>

Spring onto the balls of both feet with R foot in front of L	1
Spring onto the balls of both feet with L foot in front of R	2
Tap step L	&3
Tap step R	&4
Tap step L	&5
Shuffle R	&6
Ball dig R (with weight) Heel beat R	&7
Shuffle L	&&
Ball dig L (with weight) Heel beat L	a8
Spring onto the balls of both feet with L foot in front of R	1
Spring onto the balls of both feet with R foot in front of L	2
Tap step R	&3
Tap step L	&4
Tap step R	&5
Shuffle L	&6
Ball dig L (with weight) Heel beat L	&7
Shuffle R	&&
Ball dig R (with weight) Heel beat R	a8

Continued/

I
N
T
E
R
M
E
D
I
A
T
E

/continued

Spring onto the balls of both feet with R foot in
  front of L   1

Spring onto the balls of both feet with L foot in
  front of R   2

Tap step L   &3

Tap step R   &4

Tap step L   &5

Shuffle R   &6

Ball dig R (with weight) Heel beat R   &7

Shuffle L   &&

Ball dig L (with weight) Heel beat L   a8

Break R commencing with 'Hop L' instead of
'Step L' to continue break on the correct side   2 bars

Repeat all on opposite side   8 bars

163

<u>Swanee river</u> (with variation)

Step L	1
Shuffle R Step R	&a2
Shuffle L Step L	&a3
Spring onto both feet with R foot in front of L	4
Hop L	5
Heel dig R Step L	&6
Ball dig R (with weight) Step L	&7
Spring onto both feet with R foot in front of L	8
Step R	1
Shuffle L Step L	&a2
Shuffle R Step R	&a3
Spring onto both feet with L foot in front of R	4
Hop R	5
Heel dig L Step R	&6
Ball dig L (with weight) Step R	&7
Spring onto both feet with L foot in front of R	8

Continued/

/continued

Variation -

Step L	1
Heel dig R Step L	&2
Ball dig R (with weight) Step L	&3
Spring onto both feet with R foot in front of L	4
Step R	5
Heel dig L Step R	&6
Ball dig L (with weight) Step R	&7
Spring onto both feet with L foot in front of R	8

Break R · 2 bars

Repeat all on opposite side · 8 bars

INTERMEDIATE

165

SINGLE &
DOUBLE
JUMPS

<u>Swanee walking</u> (with variation)

Step L	1
Shuffle R Step R	&a2
Shuffle L Step L	&a3
Spring onto both feet with R foot in front of L	4

Travelling forwards -

Hop L	5
Shuffle R Step R	&a6
Tap step L	&7
Brush R forward	&
Heel beat L	8

Travelling backwards -

Step R	1
Shuffle L Step L	&a2
Shuffle R Step R	&a3
Spring onto both feet with L foot in front of R	4

Travelling forwards -

Hop R	5
Shuffle L Step L	&a6
Tap step R	&7
Brush L forward	&
Heel beat R	8

Continued/

/continued

Variation -

Tap step L backwards	&1
Tap step R backwards	&2
Tap step L forwards	&3
Brush R forward	&
Heel beat L	4
Tap step R backwards	&5
Tap step L backwards	&6
Tap step R forwards	&7
Brush L forward	&
Heel beat R	8
Break – R	2 bars
Repeat all on opposite side	8 bars

I
N
T
E
R
M
E
D
I
A
T
E

167

NO
CATEGORY

Single & double heel down
(with variation)

INTERMEDIATE

Step L	1
Heel dig R (no weight) Heel dig R (with weight)	&a
Step L	2
Shuffle R	&a
Step R	3
Heel dig L (no weight) Heel dig L (with weight)	&a
Step R	4
Shuffle L	&a
Step L	5
Heel dig R (no weight) Heel dig R (with weight)	&a
Step L	6
Ball dig R (no weight) Ball dig R (with weight)	&a
Step L	7
Heel dig R (no weight) Heel dig R (with weight)	&a
Step L	8
Shuffle R	&a

Continued/

/continued

Step R	1
Heel dig L (no weight) Heel dig L (with weight)	&a
Step R	2
Shuffle L	&a
Step L	3
Heel dig R (no weight) Heel dig R (with weight)	&a
Step L	4
Shuffle R	&a
Step R	5
Heel dig L (no weight) Heel dig L (with weight)	&a
Step R	6
Ball dig L (no weight) Ball dig L (with weight)	&a
Step R	7
Heel dig L (no weight) Heel dig L (with weight)	&a
Step R	8
Shuffle L	&a

INTERMEDIATE

continued/

NO
CATEGORY

/continued

<u>Variation</u> -

Step L	1
Heel dig R (no weight) Heel dig R (with weight)	&a
Step L	2
Ball dig R (no weight) Ball dig R (with weight)	&a
Step L	3
Heel dig R (no weight) Heel dig R (with weight)	&a
Step L	4
Shuffle R	&a
Step R	5
Heel dig L (no weight) Heel dig L (with weight)	&a
Step R	6
Ball dig L (no weight) Ball dig L (with weight)	&a
Step R	7
Heel dig L (no weight) Heel dig L (with weight)	&a
Step R	8
Shuffle L	&a
Break – R	2 bars
Repeat all on opposite side	8 bars

Straight tap, double heel down & double shuffle

(Repeats 6 times on alternate sides)

Step L	1
Straight tap R in place	&
Step R Step L	a2
Heel dig R (no weight) Heel dig R (with weight)	&a
Step L	3
Shuffle R Hop L	&a4
Shuffle R	&a
Step R	5
Straight tap L in place	&
Step L Step R	a6
Heel dig L (no weight) Heel dig L (with weight)	&a
Step R	7
Shuffle L Hop R	&a8
Shuffle L	&a
Step L	1
Straight tap R in place	&
Step R Step L	a2
Heel dig R (no weight) Heel dig R (with weight)	&a
Step L	3
Shuffle R Hop L	&a4
Shuffle R	&a

I N T E R M E D I A T E

Continued/

171

/continued

Step R	5
Straight tap L in place	&
Step L Step R	a6
Heel dig L (no weight) Heel dig L (with weight)	&a
Step R	7
Shuffle L Hop R	&a8
Shuffle L	&a
Step L	1
Straight tap R in place	&
Step R Step L	a2
Heel dig R (no weight) Heel dig R (with weight)	&a
Step L	3
Shuffle R Hop L	&a4
Shuffle R	&a
Step R	5
Straight tap L in place	&
Step L Step R	a6
Heel dig L (no weight) Heel dig L (with weight)	&a
Step R	7
Shuffle L Hop R	&a8
Shuffle L	&a
Break R	2 bars
Repeat all on opposite side	8 bars

INTERMEDIATE

172

Straight tap, double heel down & 2 straight taps

(Repeats 6 times on alternate sides)

Step L	1
Straight tap R in place	&
Step R Step L	a2
Heel dig R (no weight) Heel dig R (with weight)	&a
Step L	3
Shuffle R Hop L	&a4
2 Straight taps R in place	&a
Step R	5
Straight tap L in place	&
Step L Step R	a6
Heel dig L (no weight) Heel dig L (with weight)	&a
Step R	7
Shuffle L Hop R	&a8
2 Straight taps L in place	&a
Step L	1
Straight tap R in place	&
Step R Step L	a2
Heel dig R (no weight) Heel dig R (with weight)	&a
Step L	3
Shuffle R Hop L	&a4
2 Straight taps R in place	&a

INTERMEDIATE

Continued/

173

/continued

Step R	5
Straight tap L in place	&
Step L Step R	a6
Heel dig L (no weight) Heel dig L (with weight)	&a
Step R	7
Shuffle L Hop R	&a8
2 Straight taps L in place	&a
Step L	1
Straight tap R in place	&
Step R Step L	a2
Heel dig R (no weight) Heel dig R (with weight)	&a
Step L	3
Shuffle R Hop L	&a4
2 Straight taps R in place	&a
Step R	5
Straight tap L in place	&
Step L Step R	a6
Heel dig L (no weight) Heel dig L (with weight)	&a
Step R	7
Shuffle L Hop R	&a8
2 Straight taps L in place	&a
Break R	2 bars
Repeat all on opposite side	8 bars

Double heel down & double treble
(with variation)

Step L	1
Heel dig R (no weight) Heel dig R (with weight)	&a
Step L	2
Shuffle R	&a
Step R	3
Heel dig L (no weight) Heel dig L (with weight)	&a
Step R	4
Shuffle L	&a
Spring L Shuffle R	5&&
Step R-L	a6
Shuffle R Double treble R	&a
Hop L Shuffle R	7&&
Step R-L	a8
Shuffle R	&a

I N T E R M E D I A T E

Continued/

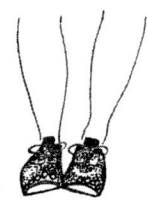

175

NO
CATEGORY

/continued

Step R	1
Heel dig L (no weight) Heel dig L (with weight)	&a
Step R	2
Shuffle L	&a
Step L	3
Heel dig R (no weight) Heel dig R (with weight)	&a
Step L	4
Shuffle R	&a

Spring R Shuffle L ⎫   5&&
Step L-R | a6
Shuffle L   ⎬ Double treble L &a
Hop R Shuffle L | 7&&
Step L-R | a8
Shuffle L   ⎭   &a

continued/

/continued

<u>Variation</u> –

Spring L Shuffle R	⎫	1&&
Step R-L		a2
Shuffle R	Double treble R	&a
Hop L Shuffle R		3&&
Step R-L		a4
Shuffle R	⎭	&a

Spring R Shuffle L	⎫	5&&
Step L-R		a6
Shuffle L	Double treble L	&a
Hop R Shuffle L		7&&
Step L-R		a8
Shuffle L	⎭	&a

Break R   2 bars

Repeat all on opposite side   8 bars

I N T E R M E D I A T E

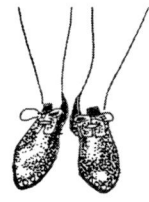

177

Double heel down & elevated side clip
(heel to heel)

Step L	1
Heel dig R (no weight) Heel dig R (with weight)	&a
Step L	2
Shuffle R	&a
Step R	3
Heel dig L (no weight) Heel dig L (with weight)	&a
Step R	4
Shuffle L	&a
Step L & raise R leg to R side	5(&)
Hop L & clip R heel with L heel (inside of heels	
touching)	a6
Step R & raise L leg to L side	7(&)
Hop R & clip L heel with R heel (inside of heels	
touching)	a8

INTERMEDIATE

Continued/

/continued

Step L	1
Heel dig R (no weight) Heel dig R (with weight)	&a
Step L	2
Shuffle R	&a
Step R	3
Heel dig L (no weight) Heel dig L (with weight)	&a
Step R	4
Shuffle L	&a
Step L & raise R leg to R side	5(&)
Hop L & clip R heel with L heel (inside of heels touching)	a6
Step R & raise L leg to L side	7(&)
Hop R & clip L heel with R heel (inside of heels touching)	a8

INTERMEDIATE

continued/

179

NO
CATEGORY

/continued

Step L	1
Heel dig R (no weight) Heel dig R (with weight)	&a
Step L	2
Shuffle R	&a
Step R	3
Heel dig L (no weight) Heel dig L (with weight)	&a
Step R	4
Shuffle L	&a
Step L & raise R leg to R side	5(&)
Hop L & clip R heel with L heel (inside of heels touching)	a6
Step R & raise L leg to L side	7(&)
Hop R & clip L heel with R heel (inside of heels touching)	a8
Break R	2 bars
Repeat all on opposite side	8 bars

<u>Shuffle</u>

R side –

Step L	1
Shuffle R Step R	&a2
Shuffle L Step L	&a3
Shuffle R	(&)a4
Hop L Heel beat L	&a
Step R behind	5
Tap step L	&6
Shuffle R	&7
Hop L Heel beat L	&a
Ball dig R in place	8

L side –

Step R	1
Shuffle L Step L	&a2
Shuffle R Step R	&a3
Shuffle L	(&)a4
Hop R Heel beat R	&a
Step L behind	5
Tap step R	&6
Shuffle L	&7
Hop R Heel beat R	&a
Ball dig L in place	8

**I
N
T
E
R
M
E
D
I
A
T
E**

181

Double shuffle & twizzle slap

R side -

Step L	1
Shuffle R Hop L Shuffle R	&a2&a
Step R	3
Shuffle L Hop R Shuffle L	&a4&a
Step L	5
Shuffle R twice (4 beat single twizzle)	(&)a6&a
Brush R forward	7
Slap R	8

L side –

Step R	1
Shuffle L Hop R Shuffle L	&a2&a
Step L	3
Shuffle R Hop L Shuffle R	&a4&a
Step R	5
Shuffle L twice (4 beat single twizzle)	(&)a6&a
Brush L forward	7
Slap L	8

INTERMEDIATE

Stamp & twizzle slap

R side –

Step L	1
Straight tap R	2
Shuffle R	&3
Ball dig R (with weight) Heel beat R	&a
Ball dig L	4
Step L	5
Shuffle R twice (4 beat single twizzle)	(&)a6&a
Brush forward R	7
Slap R	8

L side -

Step R	1
Straight tap L	2
Shuffle L	&3
Ball dig L (with weight) Heel beat L	&a
Ball dig R	4
Step R	5
Shuffle L twice (4 beat single twizzle)	(&)a6&a
Brush forward L	7
Slap L	8

INTERMEDIATE

Stamp & clip toes & heels together twice

R side –

Step L	1
Straight tap R	2
Shuffle R	&3
Ball dig R (with weight) Heel beat R	&a
Ball dig L	4
Heel dig L-R	&a
Clip toes together	5
Step L-R	&a
Clip heels together	6
Heel dig L-R	&a
Clip toes together	7
Step L-R	&a
Clip heels together	8

Continued/

INTERMEDIATE

/continued

L side -

Step R	1
Straight tap L	2
Shuffle L	&3
Ball dig L (with weight) Heel beat L	&a
Ball dig R	4
Heel dig R-L	&a
Clip toes together	5
Step R-L	&a
Clip heels together	6
Heel dig R-L	&a
Clip toes together	7
Step R-L	&a
Clip heels together	8

INTERMEDIATE

Stamp, clip toes together twice & clip heels together once

R side –

Step L	1
Straight tap R	2
Shuffle R	&3
Ball dig R (with weight) Heel beat R	&a
Ball dig L	4
Heel dig L-R	&5
Clip toes together twice	(&)a6
Step L-R	&7
Clip heels together once	8

L side -

Step R	1
Straight tap L	2
Shuffle L	&3
Ball dig L (with weight) Heel beat L	&a
Ball dig R	4
Heel dig R-L	&5
Clip toes together twice	(&)a6
Step R-L	&7
Clip heels together once	8

INTERMEDIATE

Double jump & twizzle slap

R side –

Spring onto the balls of both feet with R foot in front of L	1
Spring onto the balls of both feet with L foot in front of R	2
Tap step L	&3
Tap step R	&4
Step L	5
Shuffle R twice (4 beat single twizzle)	(&)a6&a
Brush forward R	7
Slap R	8

L side –

Spring onto the balls of both feet with L foot in front of R	1
Spring onto the balls of both feet with R foot in front of L	2
Tap step R	&3
Tap step L	&4
Step R	5
Shuffle L twice (4 beat single twizzle)	(&)a6&a
Brush forward L	7
Slap L	8

INTERMEDIATE

<u>Double jump & toe to heel clip</u>

R side –

Spring onto the balls of both feet with R foot in front of L	1
Spring onto the balls of both feet with L foot in front of R	2
Tap step L	&3
Tap step R	&4
Heel dig L	5
Toe clip R to L heel	&
Step R behind L	a
Step L in place	6
Toe clip R to L heel	&
Heel beat L	a
Shuffle R	7&
Heel beat L	a
Ball dig R in place	8

Continued/

Vertical margin text: INTERMEDIATE

/continued

L side –

Spring onto the balls of both feet with L foot in front of R	1
Spring onto the balls of both feet with R foot in front of L	2
Tap step R	&3
Tap step L	&4
Heel dig R	5
Toe clip L to R heel	&
Step L behind R	a
Step R in place	6
Toe clip L to R heel	&
Heel beat R	a
Shuffle L	7&
Heel beat R	a
Ball dig L in place	8

I
N
T
E
R
M
E
D
I
A
T
E

Double jump & clip toes & heels together twice

R side –

Spring onto the balls of both feet with R foot in front of L	1
Spring onto the balls of both feet with L foot in front of R	2
Tap step L	&3
Tap step R	&4
Heel dig L Heel dig R	&a
Clip toes together	5
Step onto the balls of the feet L-R	&a
Clip heels together	6
Heel dig L Heel dig R	&a
Clip toes together	7
Step L-R	&a
Clip heels together	8

Continued/

/continued

L side –

Spring onto the balls of both feet with L foot in front of R	1
Spring onto the balls of both feet with R foot in front of L	2
Tap step R	&3
Tap step L	&4
Heel dig R Heel dig L	&a
Clip toes together	5
Step onto the balls of the feet R-L	&a
Clip heels together	6
Heel dig R Heel dig L	&a
Clip toes together	7
Step R-L	&a
Clip heels together	8

I N T E R M E D I A T E

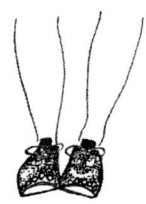

191

Straight tap, double heel down on alternate sides & brush forward

R side –

Step L	1
Straight tap R in place	&
Step R Step L	a2
Heel dig R (no weight) Heel dig R (with weight)	&a
Step L	3
Backward tap R	(&)a
Step R	4
Straight tap L in place	&
Step L Step R	a5
Heel dig L (no weight) Heel dig L (with weight)	&a
Step R	6
Backward tap L	(&)a
Step L	7
Brush R forward	(&)a
Heel beat L	8

INTERMEDIATE

Continued/

/continued

L side –

Step R	1
Straight tap L in place	&
Step L Step R	a2
Heel dig L (no weight) Heel dig L (with weight)	&a
Step R	3
Backward tap L	(&)a
Step L	4
Straight tap R in place	&
Step R Step L	a5
Heel dig R (no weight) Heel dig R (with weight)	&a
Step L	6
Backward tap R	(&)a
Step R	7
Brush L forward	(&)a
Heel beat R	8

I
N
T
E
R
M
E
D
I
A
T
E

Over & hop, double heel down & toe to heel clip

R side –

Step L	1
Shuffle R Hop L	&a2
Ball dig R across L (with weight) Heel beat R	&a
Step L in place	3
Ball dig R in place (with weight) Heel beat R	&a
Ball dig L	4
Step L	5
Heel dig R (no weight) Heel dig R (with weight)	&a
Heel dig L (with weight)	6
Toe clip R to L heel	&
Step R behind L	a
Step L in place	7
Toe clip R to L heel	&
Heel beat L	a
Ball dig R	8

I N T E R M E D I A T E

Continued/

/continued

L side –

Step R	1
Shuffle L Hop R	&a2
Ball dig L across R (with weight) Heel beat L	&a
Step R in place	3
Ball dig L in place (with weight) Heel beat L	&a
Ball dig R	4
Step R	5
Heel dig L (no weight) Heel dig L (with weight)	&a
Heel dig R (with weight)	6
Toe clip L to R heel	&
Step L behind R	a
Step R in place	7
Toe clip L to R heel	&
Heel beat R	a
Ball dig L	8

I N T E R M E D I A T E

BREAKS

Over & hop, double heel down & twizzles

R side –

Step L	1
Shuffle R Hop L	&a2
Ball dig R across L (with weight) Heel beat R	&a
Step L in place	3
Ball dig R in place (with weight) Heel beat R	&a
Ball dig L (with weight)	4
Heel dig R (no weight) Heel dig R (with weight)	&a
Step L	5
Shuffle R twice (4 beat single twizzle)	(&)a6&a
Ball dig R	7
Shuffle R twice (4 beat single twizzle)	(&)a8&a

L side –

Step R	1
Shuffle L Hop R	&a2
Ball dig L across R (with weight) Heel beat L	&a
Step R in place	3
Ball dig L in place (with weight) Heel beat L	&a
Ball dig R (with weight)	4
Heel dig L (no weight) Heel dig L (with weight)	&a
Step R	5
Shuffle L twice (4 beat single twizzle)	(&)a6&a
Ball dig L	7
Shuffle L twice (4 beat single twizzle)	(&)a8&a

INTERMEDIATE

Over & hop, double heel down & twizzle slap

R side –

Step L	1
Shuffle R Hop L	&a2
Ball dig R across L (with weight) Heel beat R	&a
Step L in place	3
Ball dig R in place (with weight) Heel beat R	&a
Ball dig L (with weight)	4
Heel dig R (no weight) Heel dig R (with weight)	&a
Step L	5
Shuffle R twice (4 beat single twizzle)	(&)a6&a
Brush forward R	7
Slap R	8

L side –

Step R	1
Shuffle L Hop R	&a2
Ball dig L across R (with weight) Heel beat L	&a
Step R in place	3
Ball dig L in place (with weight) Heel beat L	&a
Ball dig R (with weight)	4
Heel dig L (no weight) Heel dig L (with weight)	&a
Step R	5
Shuffle L twice (4 beat single twizzle)	(&)a6&a
Brush forward L	7
Slap L	8

INTERMEDIATE

Over & hop, clip toes & heels together & twizzle

R side –

Step L	1
Shuffle R Hop L	&a2
Ball dig R across L (with weight) Heel beat R	&a
Step L in place	3
Ball dig R in place (with weight) Heel beat R	&a
Ball dig L	4
Heel dig L-R	&a
Clip toes together	5
Step L-R	&a
Clip heels together	6
Step L	7
Shuffle R twice (4 beat single twizzle)	(&)a8&a

Continued/

I
N
T
E
R
M
E
D
I
A
T
E

/continued

L side –

Step R	1
Shuffle L Hop R	&a2
Ball dig L across R (with weight) Heel beat L	&a
Step R in place	3
Ball dig L in place (with weight) Heel beat L	&a
Ball dig R	4
Heel dig R-L	&a
Clip toes together	5
Step R-L	&a
Clip heels together	6
Step R	7
Shuffle L twice (4 beat single twizzle)	(&)a8&a

I N T E R M E D I A T E

BREAKS

Stepping over, clip toes together & twizzle

R side –

Tap step L	&1
Shuffle R	&2
Ball dig R across (with weight) Heel beat R	&a
Step L	3
Tap step R in place	&4
Heel dig L-R	&a
Clip toes together	5
Step L	6
Shuffle R twice (4 beat single twizzle)	(&)a7&a
Ball dig R	8

L side –

Tap step R	&1
Shuffle L	&2
Ball dig L across (with weight) Heel beat L	&a
Step R	3
Tap step L in place	&4
Heel dig R-L	&a
Clip toes together	5
Step R	6
Shuffle L twice (4 beat single twizzle)	(&)a7&a
Ball dig L	8

INTERMEDIATE

<u>Walking Monty</u>

R side –

Tap step L	&1
Shuffle R	&2
Ball dig R across (with weight) Heel beat R	&a
Step L	3
Tap step R in place	&4
Tap step L	&5
Ball dig R behind (with weight)	(&)a
Heel beat L	6
Shuffle R twice (4 beat single twizzle)	(&)a7&a
Ball dig R	8

L side –

Tap step R	&1
Shuffle L	&2
Ball dig L across (with weight) Heel beat L	&a
Step R	3
Tap step L in place	&4
Tap step R	&5
Ball dig L behind (with weight)	(&)a
Heel beat R	6
Shuffle L twice (4 beat single twizzle)	(&)a7&a
Ball dig L	8

I
N
T
E
R
M
E
D
I
A
T
E

<u>Happy wanderer</u>

R side –

Shuffle L	&&
Ball dig L (with weight) Heel beat L	a1
Forward tap R Heel beat L	&2
Shuffle R	&&
Ball dig R (with weight) Heel beat R	a3
Forward tap L Heel beat R	&4
Shuffle L Ball dig L (with weight) Heel beat L	&&a5
Shuffle R Ball dig R (with weight) Heel beat R	&&a6
Shuffle L Ball dig L (with weight) Heel beat L	&&a7
Slap R	8

L side –

Shuffle R	&&
Ball dig R (with weight) Heel beat R	a1
Forward tap L Heel beat R	&2
Shuffle L	&&
Ball dig L (with weight) Heel beat L	a3
Forward tap R Heel beat L	&4
Shuffle R Ball dig R (with weight) Heel beat R	&&a5
Shuffle L Ball dig L (with weight) Heel beat L	&&a6
Shuffle R Ball dig R (with weight) Heel beat R	&&a7
Slap L	8

I N T E R M E D I A T E

Double heel down & double treble

R side –

Step L	1
Heel dig R (no weight) Heel dig R (with weight)	&a
Step L	2
Shuffle R	&a
Step R	3
Heel dig L (no weight) Heel dig L (with weight)	&a
Step R	4
Shuffle L	&a

Spring L Shuffle R		5&&
Step R-L		a6
Shuffle R	Double treble R	&a
Hop L Shuffle R		7&&
Step R-L		a8
Shuffle R		&a

I N T E R M E D I A T E

Continued/

203

BREAKS

/continued

L side –

Step R	1
Heel dig L (no weight) Heel dig L (with weight)	&a
Step R	2
Shuffle L	&a
Step L	3
Heel dig R (no weight) Heel dig R (with weight)	&a
Step L	4
Shuffle R	&a
Spring R Shuffle L ⎫	5&&
Step L-R ⎪	a6
Shuffle L ⎬ Double treble L	&a
Hop R Shuffle L ⎪	7&&
Step L-R ⎪	a8
Shuffle L ⎭	&a

<u>Treble shuffles</u>

R side –

Spring L Shuffle R	1&&
Step R-L	a2
Shuffle R	&&
Hop L Ball dig R	a3
Spring R Shuffle L	4&&
Step L-R	a5
Spring L Shuffle R	6&&
Step R-L	a7
Slap R	8

L side –

Spring R Shuffle L	1&&
Step L-R	a2
Shuffle L	&&
Hop R Ball dig L	a3
Spring L Shuffle R	4&&
Step R-L	a5
Spring R Shuffle L	6&&
Step L-R	a7
Slap L	8

INTERMEDIATE

BREAKS

Double heel down & shuffles

R side -

Step L	1
Heel dig R (no weight) Heel dig R (with weight)	&a
Step L	2
Shuffle R	&a
Step R	3
Heel dig L (no weight) Heel dig L (with weight)	&a
Step R	4
Shuffle L	&a
Step L	5
Shuffle R	&a
Step R	6
Shuffle L	&a
Step L	7
Shuffle R	&a
Hop L	8

Continued/

/continued

L side -

Step R	1
Heel dig L (no weight) Heel dig L (with weight)	&a
Step R	2
Shuffle L	&a
Step L	3
Heel dig R (no weight) Heel dig R (with weight)	&a
Step L	4
Shuffle R	&a
Step R	5
Shuffle L	&a
Step L	6
Shuffle R	&a
Step R	7
Shuffle L	&a
Hop R	8

INTERMEDIATE

207

Single twizzle, over & hop variation & stepping back

R side –

Step L	1
Shuffle R twice (4 beat single twizzle)	(&)a2&a
Hop L	3
Ball dig R across L (with weight) Heel beat R	&a
Step L in place	4
Ball dig R in place (with weight) Heel beat R	&a
Step L	5
Shuffle R	&6
Hop L Heel beat L	&a
Step R behind L	7
Tap Step L	&8

L side –

Step R	1
Shuffle L twice (4 beat single twizzle)	(&)a2&a
Hop R	3
Ball dig L across R (with weight) Heel beat L	&a
Step R in place	4
Ball dig L in place (with weight) Heel beat L	&a
Step R	5
Shuffle L	&6
Hop R Heel beat R	&a
Step L behind R	7
Tap Step R	&8

I
N
T
E
R
M
E
D
I
A
T
E

Backward tap   With the foot raised tap the floor sharply
                      with the ball of the foot, backward & up.

Ball beat   Raise & lower the ball of the foot
                      making a downward beat onto the floor.
                      In some cases the ball of the foot is
                      already raised & therefore a downward
                      beat is achieved by simply lowering the
                      ball of the foot.

Ball dig   Dig the ball of the foot onto the floor
                      with the heel raised.   Without weight
                      unless specified.

Ball heel   A ball dig (with weight) followed by a
                      heel beat on the same foot. Ball dig &
                      heel beat together can be abbreviated to
                      "ball heel" to enable an easy flow of
                      words to fit with steps whilst practising.

Brush backward   As a backward tap but with a broader
                      movement coming from the hip.

Brush forward	As a forward tap but with a broader movement coming from the hip.	

Clip toes together	Heel dig R Heel dig L (or Heel dig L Heel dig R depending on which side of the step is being danced) & clip toes together. Weight is central on both feet.	

Clip heels together	Step onto the balls of the feet R then L (or L then R depending on which side of the step is being danced) & clip heels together. Weight is central on both feet.	

"Double heel down R"'	Step L	1
	Heel dig R (no weight)	&
	Heel dig R (with weight)	a
	Step L Shuffle R	2&a

"Double heel down L"'	Step R	1
	Heel dig L (no weight)	&
	Heel dig L (with weight)	a
	Step R Shuffle L	2&a

210

| Double shuffle R | Step L Shuffle R | 1&a |
| | Hop L Shuffle R | 2&a |

| Double shuffle L | Step R Shuffle L | 1&a |
| | Hop R Shuffle L | 2&a |

| Elevated side clip R | Raise R leg to R side & Hop L clipping R heel with L heel (inside of heels touching) |

| Elevated side clip L | Raise L leg to L side & Hop R clipping L heel with R heel (inside of heels touching) |

| Forward tap | With the foot raised tap the floor sharply with the ball of the foot, forward & up. |

| Heel beat | Raise & lower the heel making a downward beat with the heel onto the floor. In some cases the heel is already raised & therefore a downward beat is achieved by simply lowering the heel. |

211

Heel dig

Dig the heel onto the floor with the ball of the foot raised. Always with weight unless specified.

Heel to toe clip

Clip the side of the heel against the side of the toe of the other foot (wood to wood). Which side of the heel & toe is determined by the direction of the movement of the foot.

Hop

A movement of elevation on one foot landing on the ball of the same foot.

L

Left

R

Right

"Over & hop R"	Step L	1
	Shuffle R Hop L	&a2
	Ball dig R across L (with weight)	&
	Heel beat R	a
	Step L in place	3
	Ball dig R in place (with weight)	&
	Heel beat R	a
	Step L	4

"Over & hop L"	Step R	1
	Shuffle L Hop R	&a2
	Ball dig L across R (with weight)	&
	Heel beat L	a
	Step R in place	3
	Ball dig L in place (with weight)	&
	Heel beat L	a
	Step R	4

"Over & hop" variation R	Hop L	1
	Ball dig R across L (with weight)	&
	Heel beat R	a
	Step L in place	2
	Ball dig R in place (with weight)	&
	Heel beat R	a

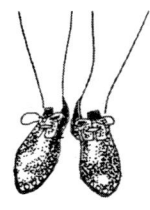

213

"Over & hop" variation L	Hop R	1
	Ball dig L across R (with weight)	&
	Heel beat L	a
	Step R in place	2
	Ball dig L in place (with weight)	&
	Heel beat L	a

Shuffle	Forward & backward tap with the same foot.

Single jump across R	Spring onto both feet with R foot in front of L foot. Weight is central on both feet.

Single jump across L	Spring onto both feet with L foot in front of R foot. Weight is central on both feet.

Slap	Raise & lower the foot in front making a heavy downbeat with the ball of the foot. (Without weight)

"Stamp R"	Step L	1
	Straight tap R	2
	Shuffle R	&3
	Ball dig R (with weight)	&
	Heel beat R	a
	Ball dig L	4

"Stamp L"	Step R	1
	Straight tap L	2
	Shuffle L	&3
	Ball dig L (with weight)	&
	Heel beat L	a
	Ball dig R	4

"Stepping back R"	Step L	1
	Shuffle R	&2
	Hop L Heel beat R	&a
	Step R behind L	3
	Tap step L in place	&4

"Stepping back L"	Step R	1
	Shuffle L	&2
	Hop R Heel beat L	&a
	Step L behind R	3
	Tap step R in place	&4

"Stepping over R"	Step L	1
	Shuffle R	&2
	Ball dig R across L (with weight)	&
	Heel beat R	a
	Step L	3
	Tap step R in place	&4

"Stepping over L"	Step R	1
	Shuffle L	&2
	Ball dig L across R (with weight)	&
	Heel beat L	a
	Step R	3
	Tap step L in place	&4

| Spring | A movement of elevation taken on one foot & landing on the ball of the other foot. |

Step	Step onto the ball of the foot in place unless otherwise indicated.
Straight tap	Tap the ball of the foot onto the floor, down & up.
Tap step	Forward tap & step onto the ball of the foot.
Toe tap	Lower & raise the tip of the toe onto the floor making a sharp beat.
Toe to heel clip	Clip the side of the toe against the side of the heel of the other foot (wood to wood). Which side of the toe & heel is determined by the direction of the movement of the foot.

Treble R – Single

Spring L Shuffle R	1&&
Step R-L	a2
Shuffle R	&a

217

Treble L – Single	Spring R Shuffle L	1&&
	Step L-R	a2
	Shuffle L	&a
Treble R – Double	Spring L Shuffle R	1&&
	Step R-L	a2
	Shuffle R	&a
	Hop L Shuffle R	3&&
	Step R-L	a4
	Shuffle R	&a
Treble L – Double	Spring R Shuffle L	1&&
	Step L-R	a2
	Shuffle L	&a
	Hop R Shuffle L	3&&
	Step L-R	a4
	Shuffle L	&a
Treble shuffle R	Spring L Shuffle R	
Treble shuffle L	Spring R Shuffle L	

Twizzle – single   2 or 3 shuffles off the same foot depending on the rhythm

Twizzle – double   5 shuffles off the same foot